THE BRIDGESTO

100 BEST
PLACES TO STAY
IN IRELAND '98

JOHN McKENNA – SALLY McKENNA

E S T R A G O N   P R E S S

FIRST PUBLISHED IN 1998

BY ESTRAGON PRESS

DURRUS

COUNTY CORK

© ESTRAGON PRESS

TEXT © JOHN & SALLY McKENNA

THE MORAL RIGHT OF THE

AUTHORS HAS BEEN ASSERTED

ISBN 1 874076 27 8

ART DIRECTION BY NICK CANN

COVER PHOTOS BY MIKE O'TOOLE

PRINTED BY COLOUR BOOKS LTD

FOR TOM HEGARTY

WITH THANKS TO...

Colm Conyngham, Nick Cann, Mike O'Toole

Ann-Marie Tobin, Des Collins, Frieda Forde, Eddie,

Pat Young, Colette Tobin, Maureen Daly, Max Harvey

Ray Buckley, Gerry Byrne, John Harold, Kevin, Ana

Caroline McGrath, Elaine Shiels

Paul & Amanada Willoughby

BRIDGESTONE

...is the world's largest tyre and rubber manufacturer.

■ Founded in Japan in 1931, it currently employs over 95,000 people in Europe, Asia and America and its products are sold in more than 150 countries. Its European plants are situated in France, Spain and Italy.

■ Bridgestone manufacture tyres for a wide variety of vehicles from passenger cars and motorcycles, trucks and buses to giant earthmovers and aircraft.

■ Many Japanese cars sold in Ireland have been fitted with Bridgestone tyres during manufacture and a host of exotic sports cars including Ferrari, Lamborghini, Porsche and Jaguar are fitted with Bridgestone performance tyres as original equipment.

■ Bridgestone commercial vehicle tyres enjoy a world-wide reputation for superior cost per kilometre performance and its aircraft tyres are used by more than 100 airlines.

■ In 1988 Bridgestone acquired the Firestone Tyre and Rubber Company combining the resources of both companies under one umbrella. This coupled with an intensive research and development programme has enabled Bridgestone to remain the world's most techno-logically advanced tyre company with testing centres in Japan, USA, Mexico and Italy.

■ Bridgestone tyres are distributed in Ireland by Bridgestone/Firestone Ireland Limited, a subsidiary of the multinational Bridgestone Corporation. A wide range of tyres are stocked in its central warehouse and staff provide sales, technical and delivery services all over the country.

■ Bridgestone tyres are available from tyre dealers throughout Ireland.

FOR FURTHER INFORMATION:

BRIDGESTONE/FIRESTONE IRELAND LTD
Unit 4
Leopardstown Office Park,
Dublin 18
Tel: (01) 295 2844
Fax: (01) 295 2858

34 Hillsborough Road,
Lisburn
BT28 1AQ
Tel: (01 846) 678331
Fax: (01 846) 673235

INTRODUCTION

Our intention with the Bridgestone Guides, and in particular with the Bridgestone 100 Best Places to Stay in Ireland, is to do our utmost to describe the spirit of both the place and the people who run it. Whilst we might concentrate more, therefore, on personalities and ambience, than on architecture and design, we take it for granted that any house which merits being in this book will be interesting from both those perspectives.

Because without good design, and an interesting architectural perspective, a house will not function properly. It will not be welcoming and hospitable. The "standard" hotel room is the best example of how monotonous design and uniformity creates a space which is hostile and uncomfortable.

Our ambition, then, is to choose the most interesting, distinguished and fun places, and to attempt to paint a word picture of the people and the houses. Sometimes, the way in which we describe a house may be somewhat oblique, but that is simply because every house is different and needs a separate approach to best describe it. A guide book which adopts a formula and sticks to it, irrespective of the different nature of each establishment, is not only innacurate, but misleading.

We hope, then, that when you walk through the door and meet your hosts and settle into your room, you might say to yourself: "Yes, this is just what I thought it would be like, and I know I am going to like it".

We know that you will like these distinguished addresses, chosen from all over Ireland. Some are lavish, some simple. Some are modern, others echo the age when they were built. All of them, however, are distinguished and congratulated by the spirit and capacity of the marvellous people who run them.

JOHN AND SALLY McKENNA
DURRUS, CO CORK

Stars - The Best

⭐

THE STARS

CO CORK
Assolas House, Kanturk
Longueville House, Mallow

CO GALWAY
Norman Villa, Galway
Quay House, Clifden

CO KERRY
The Park Hotel, Kenmare
Shelbourne Lodge, Kenmare

CO LIMERICK
The Mustard Seed at Echo Lodge, Ballingarry

CO MONAGHAN
Hilton Park, Clones

CO WEXFORD
Kelly's Resort Hotel, Rosslare

Detours - worth going far out of your way

THE DETOURS
CO CORK
Fortview House, Goleen
Liss Ard Lake Lodge, Skibbereen

CO DUBLIN
Chestnut Lodge, Monkstown
No 31, Dublin

CO WEXFORD
Salville House, Enniscorthy

HOW TO USE THIS BOOK

■ The Bridgestone 100 Best Places to Stay in Ireland is arranged **ALPHABETICALLY, BY COUNTY** so it begins with County Carlow, which is followed by County Cavan, and so on.

■ Within the counties, the entries are once again listed alphabetically, so Aherne's, in Youghal, East Cork, is followed by Assolas House, in Kanturk, North Cork.

■ Entries in Northern Ireland are itemised together, at the end of the book.

■ The contents of the Bridgestone 100 Best Guides are exclusively the result of the authors' deliberations. All meals and accommodation were paid for and any offers of discounts or gifts were refused.

■ Many of the places featured in this book are only open during the summer season, which means that they can be closed for any given length of time between October and March. Many others change their opening times during the winter.

■ **PRICES:** Average prices are calculated on the basis of one night's stay for bed and breakfast. Look out for special offers for weekends, several day's stay, or off season.

■ **CREIT CARDS:** Most houses take major credit cards, particularly the Visa, Access/Master group. Check if you intend to use American Express or Diners Card. If a house does not accept credit cards, this is indicated in the notes section of their entry.

■ Finally, we greatly appreciate receiving reports, suggestions and criticisms from readers, and would like to thank those who have written in the past, whose opinions are of enormous assistance to us when considering which 100 places to stay finally make it into this book.

CONTENTS

KILGRANEY COUNTRY HOUSE
Bryan Leech & Martin Marley
Bagenalstown, Co Carlow
Tel: (0503) 75283 Fax: 75283

Bryan Leech and Martin Marley's darling house, Kilgraney, is one of the cult destinations in Ireland. What explains the attraction? One might describe it as a knowingness, a richly textured and appreciated sense of irony, which infuses both the design and the loveable cooking. The forbidding exterior of this 1820 house, so severely Protestant at first sight, merely serves to accentuate the playfulness which the interior enjoys, a warm and witty space, but one which never sacrifices comfort for style.

Whilst the public rooms are alluringly welcoming, the five bedrooms are assuredly private and enveloping. But design only plays one part in explaining Kilgraney's success. Of course, people love its beauty, and its proximity to Dublin, but the final pillar of this noble establishment is excellent cooking.

It's modern cooking, as likely to offer black beans with salmon as to offer pesto with the fish, as likely to see a meal start with a roast garlic custard or a warm lamb salad with lime leaf, but it is centred firmly on generous flavours and a true understanding of how to make a meal enjoyable, and Bryan Leech knows how to use flavours for both balance and counterpoint.

● **OPEN:**
Jun-Aug weekly,
Mar-May & Sept-Oct Weekends
● **ROOMS:**
Five rooms, four en-suite
● **AVERAGE PRICE:**
B&B £30-£35 per person sharing, £25 single
(£10 single supplement, high season only)

● **NOTES:**
Dinner 8pm, £22, communal table, book by noon
(separate tables by request – limited)
No Wheelchair Access. Enclosed car parking
Children – under 12 by arrangement only
● Just off the R705 (L18), 3.5 miles (6km) from
Bagenalstown (Muine Bheag) on the road heading
towards Borris.

LISNAMANDRA HOUSE
Bert & Iris Neill
Crossdoney, Co Cavan
Tel: (049) 37196 Fax: 37111

The Neills' farmhouse lies just south of the rich complex of lakes of County Cavan's Erne System. It has long been one of the most respected and admired of Irish B&B's, patronised each year by folk who have been often but can't get quite enough of the true hospitality and warmth and thoughtfulness of the house.

"I have tried altering the breakfast menu a couple of times", Iris Neill says. "But everybody comes back looking for the same things!". And who could blame them. For whilst the list of options for breakfast in Bert and Iris Neill's celebrated Bed and Breakfast is just about as long as a city telephone directory, it sure is a heck of a lot more interesting.

Telephone directories don't offer you porridge, for a start. They don't furnish perfectly grilled black and white pudding, and couldn't get you a piece of gammon for love nor money. They wouldn't think of matching poached eggs with waffles, or scrambled eggs with mushrooms, and history has yet to document an episode where a telephone directory brought you some pancakes and maple syrup on a plate first thing in the morning. And there's more: french toast, grilled tomato, grilled kippers on toast, on and on it goes, happily ending with the Falstaffian promise of: "Any combination of the above".

● **OPEN:**
May-Oct
● **ROOMS:**
Six rooms, 4 en suite, 2 sharing 1 bathroom
● **AVERAGE PRICE:**
B&B £15-£17 per person sharing

● **NOTES:**
No Dinner
Enclosed Car Park
No Wheelchair Access
Children – high chairs, cots
● Leave Cavan on the Crossdoney Road, and Lisnamandra House is clearly signposted almost five miles from the town.

MacNEAN TOWNHOUSE
Joe & Vera Maguire
Blacklion
Co Cavan
Tel: (072) 53022
Fax: 53404

One of these days, people will begin to discover the so-far undiscovered glories of the border counties like Cavan, Leitrim and Monaghan.

But, so far, apart from anglers and a few others, that has not happened, which makes touring the area a delight. Indeed, County Cavan seems in many ways to have been not just overlooked, but forgotten, by the passage of time. There is none of the tawdry new style of housing and building which is despoiling other parts of the country. Touring here is a step back in time.

So, if you really want to get away from it all, Cavan it is, and the MacNean Townhouse it is. Young Neven Maguire cooks in the family restaurant, the MacNean Bistro, and he cooks with a brilliance which is enthralling.

His food, alone, is reason to come to Blacklion – indeed it is the reason why most folk come here in the first place – and the rooms the family offer in the house are small but cosy and comfy. They are thoughtful, the Maguire family, and want to make sure you have what you want and what you need. And you can say you were here before everyone else.

● **OPEN:**
All year, except Xmas
● **ROOMS:**
Six rooms
all en-suite
● **AVERAGE PRICE:**
B&B £20 per person sharing
£23 single

● **NOTES:**
Dinner 6pm-9pm, £25
No Wheelchair Access
Children – welcome
high chair, cot
● On the main street in Blacklion.

CAHERBOLANE FARMHOUSE
Sinead Cahill
Corofin, Co Clare
Tel: (065) 37638

Patricia Cahill, who now runs the excellent Flappers Restaurant, in Tulla, put Caherbolane on the map with her cooking, and her sister Sinead and mum, Brid, are continuing the family tradition.

Caherbolane is a simple farmhouse, but the second you step inside the door and the Cahills take you under their wing, you are destined to have a good time.

You can meet people staying here who almost seem to be in a daze of delight.

It isn't just the fine food cooked by Sinead Cahill and her mum, Brid, they explain, and it isn't just the simple, comfy rooms, and it isn't just the good crack... it's just that it is so unlikely... to be here in a modest farmhouse in County Clare... and to be able to enjoy such delicious and devoted cooking with such pure flavours and such precise execution... at such modest prices... and the Cahills are so nice... and yes let's have the full Irish breakfast in the morning... A delirium of happiness.

If there is such a state, then it is because the Cahills understand those flavours and savours from food which are best at cranking our pleasure dials to the max. Lovely.

● **OPEN:**
Easter-Oct
● **ROOMS:**
Four rooms, one en suite
● **AVERAGE PRICE:**
B&B £16 per person sharing
£17 en suite, £5 single supplement

● **NOTES:**
Dinner 7pm-9pm, £16. Bring Your Own Wine
Enclosed car parking
No Wheelchair Access
Children – welcome, high chair
● Caherbolane is signposted from Corofin. Take the Gort road, and travel one and a half km out of the village, turn at the signpost and travel a further three and a half km.

CLIFDEN HOUSE
Jim & Bernadette Robson
Corofin
Co Clare
Tel: (065) 37692
Fax: 37692

"We found the house slipping gracefully into ruin twenty years ago. Since then, little by little, we have brought it back to life with our own hands and the laughter of our friends", write Jim and bernadette Robson.

"The work is not finished nor will it be twenty years hence, but we have restored much of the property following the criteria of respecting its tradition of hospitality and the comfort of our friends and guests".

The Robsons' task is a noble one, and a major challenge, for Clifden is a fine big house, a Georgian mansion of imposing mien, set hard by the shore of Lake Inchiquin.

The work to the house is being done by the Robsons themselves, patiently, piecemeal, bit-by-bit, room-by-room. They are confident with the colours chosen for the bedrooms, and there is a keen decorator's eye evident.

But it is not complete yet, and won't be for some time, which some cautious souls may find off putting.

But, if you are bold at heart, and enjoy spirited people and the ageless charms of a secreted-away house – this is truly a hidden place, despite its proximity to Corofin – Clifden may be the very place you are looking for.

● **OPEN:**
All year, except Xmas
● **ROOMS:**
Four rooms, all en suite
● **AVERAGE PRICE:**
B&B £35 per person

● **NOTES:**
No Credit Cards accepted
Dinner 8pm, £18, communal table
Enclosed car parking
No Wheelchair Access
Children – welcome, cot, high chair, babysitting on prior request
● Left of the grotto in the village, second right, then first right into the drive.

FERGUS VIEW
Mary Kelleher
Kilnaboy, Corofin, Co Clare
Tel: (065) 37606 Fax: 37192
e-mail: deckell@indigo.ie

Fergus View is a landmark house. Mary Kelleher's house is, firstly, a landmark for hospitality – that lovely, easy, capable, Clare hospitality – and for fine, fine food. Mrs Kelleher's food is one of those styles which we can describe as achieving the perfection of domestic cooking, and all of her culinary work is suffused with the desire to make a meal enticing and satisfying.

Turbot with a black peppercorn sauce. Roast stuffed pork steak with a sweet-sour sauce. A casserole of lamb with a honey and orange sauce, with fresh celery and carrots. Salmon en papilotte with fresh herbs. Vegetables and herbs have come from no further than the garden, so their vigour is bounteous: potatoes au gratin with Poulcoin cheese. Piperonata. Buttered garden leeks. The local foods, in the local house.

Desserts are fun, sticky things: rich lemon cheesecake decorated with lemon scented geranium leaves; blackberry and apple tart; meringue nest with seasonal marinated berries.

Breakfast, meantime, offers another feast: Kilnaboy goat's cheese with mushrooms and bacon on a toast base; crêpes with kiwi fruit and maple syrup; smoked kippers with tomato; a bumper breakfast of bacon with true free-range eggs. Utterly delightful.

- **OPEN:**
Easter-1 Oct
- **ROOMS:**
Six rooms, five en suite
- **AVERAGE PRICE:**
£16.50-£18.50 per person sharing
£6-£11 single supplement

- **NOTES:**
Dinner 6.30pm, book by noon, £15.50
Enclosed car parking. No Wheelchair Access
Children – high chairs, cot, babysitting
- Take the road north from Corofin, heading towards Kilnaboy. The house is 2 miles north of Corofin, on the left hand side, 100m from Kilnaboy Medieval church.

ADELE'S
Adele Connor
Adele's Bakery
Schull, Co Cork
Tel: (028) 28459
Fax: 28865

Adele's was, once upon a time, a bank. A simple quartet of rooms up the narrow stairs above the café, the place appeals – somehow, someway – to some sort of youthful idea of freedom and simplicity, the same sort of shackle-breaking urge which propelled you to hoist a rucksack onto your back when you were seventeen and take off for European sights seen from European trains.

Whether or not you actually are seventeen and an ardent Eurorailer with a rucksack, or have added a further seventeen years or more to the time when you were seventeen and now travel in a carriage built for four, Adele's suits all ages. Simple beds, simple boards on the floor, a shared bathroom, it fulfills the need for a functional, effective pensione, somewhere from where you can stake out the pubs and eateries of Schull, a village of minuscule size and maximum fascination.

The fact that the rooms are above one of the very best cafés in the country, and that the smells of coffee and fresh bread are likely to rouse you from your dreams of youth to enjoy a terrific breakfast, is not something to be taken lightly.

● **OPEN:**
Easter-Halloween, Xmas & New Year
● **ROOMS:**
Four rooms, sharing one shower-room
● **AVERAGE PRICE:**
B&B £12.50 per person
● **CREDIT CARDS:**
Visa, Access/Master

● **NOTES:**
Bakery, Café open all day
Dinner Easter & high summer
7pm-10.30pm, £10-£17
No Wheelchair Access
Children – welcome, high chair, cot
● On the main street in Schull, at the top of the hill, opposite the AIB bank.

AHERNE'S

The Fitzgibbon family
163 North Main Street
Youghal, Co Cork
Tel: (024) 92424
Fax: 93633
e-mail: ahe@iol.ie

There is a happy sense of timelessness about this Youghal legend. It may be created by the fact that it is currently the third generation of the Fitzgibbon family who run this handsome place, but it may equally be the sense of true professionalism and seriousness of purpose which the family espouse and practice.

Their hard work means that each and every year new followers are added to the fold of those for whom the Fitzgibbon family's organisation spells bliss itself. Charmed by the intimacy of the dining room, succoured by the comfort of the food, lulled by the promise of the wine list and buffeted by the grand charms of the bedrooms, they speak afterwards in enraptured tones.

The comfort of Aherne's is enveloping. Whether you are swaddling in one of its large bedrooms, caught up in the deliciously immediate enjoyment of a quiet, sumptuous breakfast, or simply quietly sitting in front of the big turf-burning fire, this is where you want to be. No-one, it seems, is immune to the charms of the pinky, art-decked dining room, or the cosy bar where you are left alone to drink in the atmosphere.

● **OPEN:**
All year
● **ROOMS:**
Twelve rooms, All en suite
● **AVERAGE PRICE:**
B&B from £60 per person sharing
£20 single supplement

● **NOTES:**
Dinner 6.30pm-9.30pm Mon-Sun, £25
Bar food also available
Enclosed car parking
Full Wheelchair Access
Children – welcome, high chair, cot, babysitting
● Well signposted as you approach Youghal from any direction.

ASSOLAS COUNTRY HOUSE ✪
Joe & Hazel Bourke
Kanturk, Co Cork
Tel: (029) 50015 Fax: 50795
assolas@tinet.it

Assolas is a place unto itself, a little republic of pleasure. Set a few miles from the nondescript town of Kanturk, it is one of the great Irish country houses, arguably the greatest.

It is dashingly romantic, at night when the house is dappled with lights and you wander alongside the river. It is beautiful on a warm north Cork morning, as you walk down to the herb garden and amidst the sprucely manicured hedges and shrubs.

It is welcoming, thanks to Joe and Hazel Bourke and their youthful energy, their easy wit and style. Mrs Bourke cooks, and she does so with a great feeling for both flavour and texture in a dish, and adds an organic appreciation of how best to exploit the fresh herbs, many of them grown out back in Assolas' vegetable garden.

Such wonderful food, enjoyed in the quiet comfort of the red-walled dining room, makes you doubly glad to be at Assolas and, days after, images from the visit come back into the mind: the whites-clad cook crossing the lawn after collecting herbs; the sea-green colour of a bowl of asparagus soup; the bursting orange and red colours of a breakfast compote; the comfort of the rooms.

● **OPEN:**
end Mar-Nov
● **ROOMS:**
Nine rooms, all en suite
● **AVERAGE PRICE:**
B&B £44-£82 per person sharing
£11 & £17 single supplement

● **NOTES:**
Dinner 7pm-8.30pm, £30
No Wheelchair Access
Enclosed Car Parking
Children – welcome, high chair, cot
● Take the N72 Mallow/Killarney Road, and 10km west of Mallow you will see the first signpost at a small junction.

BALLYMAKEIGH HOUSE
Margaret Browne
Killeagh
Co Cork
Tel: (024) 95184
Fax: 95370

Margaret Browne has become something of a celebrity since writing a collection of her recipes which she cooks in Ballymakeigh, and appearing here and there on television. Effervescent, bubbly, irrepressible, she is a t.v. producer's dream, with a constant flow of banter and good humour a mainstay of her work.

But her true fame has always rested with her work in her lovely farmhouse, just off the main road between Cork and the east, up on the hill above the village of Killeagh. It has long been one of the best-known, and best-loved, B&B's in the entire country.

Margaret Browne is one more of those formidable women who orchestrate B&Bs in the midst of doing so much other work that the mere thought of such toil is exhausting, never mind the reality. In the process she has reaped accolades galore, and anyone who has stayed here quickly sees why; you are looked after so, so well.

For travellers this location in east County Cork allows one to roam up to the ever mysterious beauty of The Vee, or down to the beaches and the kiss-me-quick giggliness of Trabolgan or Ardmore, before returning to a fine dinner which will feature garden vegetables and herbs.

● **OPEN:**
All year, except Xmas
● **ROOMS:**
Five rooms, all en suite
● **AVERAGE PRICE:**
B&B £25-£30 per person sharing
£5 single supplement

● **NOTES:**
Dinner 8pm, £22.50, separate tables
No Wheelchair Access
Enclosed Car Parking
Children – welcome, high chair, cot, babysitting
● Signposted on the N25, 6 miles west of Youghal. Look out for the Old Thatch in Killeagh.

BALLYMALOE HOUSE
The Allen family
Shanagarry, Midleton
Co Cork
Tel: (021) 652531
Fax: 652021
e-mail: bmaloe@iol.ie

The vision of Myrtle Allen, Ballymaloe's guiding spirit, is fundamentally a mix of the aesthetic and the ascetic, and Ballymaloe's secret is to balance one with the other.

If you let yourself fall captive to its quiet spell, then you will come to understand how it has acquired its reputation. The rooms are deliberately simple, reflecting the fact that you are in a country house and not an hotel. If the staff are young, they are never less than charming. They, like everything else, are an essential part of the Ballymaloe operation, and the key to this house is the fact that they do things their own way. They do not ape or imitate. These are the things which make Ballymaloe unique.

At breakfast the bread will be oven-warm, the porridge hand-roasted, the eggs fresh from the farmyard chickens. Dinner is fine simple cooking, even the less formal Sunday night buffet, which amounts to little less than an homage to quality Irish ingredients and an Irish way of cooking them.

Don't expect the cooking to ape the creations of the culinary cutting edge – this is farmhouse cooking. Enjoy it, instead, as a place which ploughs a dedicated, devoted vision.

● **OPEN:**
All year except 24-26 Dec
● **ROOMS:**
Thirty-two rooms, all en suite
● **AVERAGE PRICE:**
B&B £55-£75 per person sharing
£20 single supplement

● **NOTES:**
Dinner 7pm-9.30pm, £31.50
Wheelchair Access
Enclosed Car Parking
Children – welcome, high chair, cot, babysitting
● Two miles beyond Cloyne, Ballycotton Rd, and well signposted in the area.

BALLYVOLANE HOUSE

Merrie and Jeremy Green
Castlelyons, Fermoy, Co Cork
Tel: (025) 36349 Fax: 36781
e-mail: ballyvol@iol.ie
website: http://www.iol.ie/ballyvolan/

Steadily and surely winning garlands now and then, Ballyvolane House is a destination deservedly becoming better known and loved. Snuggled in amidst the swollen charm of north east County Cork, one can't imagine it anywhere else.

Whilst the accommodation is professionally organised and luxurious, it never loses out on a touch of humour. Your hosts, for example, will tell you stories of a household double-murder, omitting, however, to inform you in which bedroom the terrible deed was done.

Glaring portraits of long-gone ancestors glower down at you – especially, it feels, during breakfast in the dining room – but anything ominous in their gaze is dissipated by the air of giddy, giggly fun which wraps around everyone staying here. The food, the bright fires, the gin and tonics: it's so appropriate it deserves to be satirised.

A sense of the past is with you throughout the house. In the front bedrooms, the huge baths are so deep they have to be stepped up to, and Merrie has installed a series of four decorated water closets, en-throned in twin panelled rooms, side-by-side.

Through and through, the formal surroundings of an Irish country house are never allowed to dominate over a feeling of comfort and humour.

● **OPEN:**
All year, except Xmas
● **ROOMS:**
Six rooms, Five en suite
● **AVERAGE PRICE:**
B&B £35-£45 per person sharing
£10 single supplement

● **NOTES:**
Dinner 8pm, £23, communal table
Wheelchair Access
Enclosed Car Parking
Children – welcome, high chair, cot
● Follow signs from the N8, just before Rathcormac.

BANTRY HOUSE
Brigitta & Egerton Shelswell-White
Bantry, Co Cork
Tel: (027) 50047
Fax: 50795

High, wide, and handsomely sited overlooking Bantry Bay, Bantry House is a serene architectural masterpiece. Right from the moment you arrive, it is a house which flatters your sense of well-being, flatters your sense of your own good taste.

You don't actually stay in the main part of the famous house, but in one of the wings, which has been confidently restored. And this removal from the bustle of the main house seems just right, for Bantry is the Marie Celeste of country houses, a place which seems to float along unaided, somehow.

There are, of course, people to meet and greet you at Bantry House, people to cook breakfast, to recommend the local restaurants for dinner.

But, if you wish to be alone and to evade string quartets, who pitch up here for the annual chamber music festival, and bus-borne travellers, you can hide away in the big rooms, maybe with a glass of grog you fixed yourself downstairs, and disappear into solipsism, into Garboesque grandness. All around the house things will be arranged, things will be operational, but they are done by unseen hands: the ship sails on, firmly commanded, but seemingly with no one at the helm.

● **OPEN:**
Mar-Oct
● **ROOMS:**
Nine rooms, all en suite
● **AVERAGE PRICE:**
B&B £55-£65, per person sharing
£10 single supplement

● **NOTES:**
Dinner Mon-Fri summer months, 7.30pm, £25
No Wheelchair Access
Enclosed Car Parking
Children – welcome, high chair, cot, babysitting
● From Cork follow signs to West Cork, then Bantry. The main entrance to the house is just off Bantry town square at the inner harbour.

BLAIR'S COVE HOUSE
Philippe & Sabine De Mey
Durrus, Bantry
Co Cork
Tel: (027) 61127
Fax: 61127

In the various houses and apartments which complement the acclaimed Blair's Cove Restaurant, one is able to enjoy the beauty of the detail, and the utter gorgeousness of the grander canvas.

The latter is the house's incredible location on a promontory jutting out into the lovely Dunmanus Bay. The vistas across the Sheep's Head peninsula and the Beara peninsula are awesome, the quietude of the bay itself and its wonderfully unspoilt aspect a balm for the soul.

Inside the houses, and apartments are arranged around and about the restaurant, which can be rented for self-catering or taken for shorter periods when you can avail of bed and breakfast, and which can take between two people up to eight people for the biggest house, Philippe and Sabine De Mey show the beauty of the detail.

They have an expert idea for colour and contrast and comfort, so whilst the different spaces vary wildly, they are united by an expert appreciation of how to make a space welcoming. Do note that there is also a lovely stone cottage, a few miles down the road at Goleen pier, which can also be rented, and its location is every bit as spectacular as the main house. All the spaces offer a great base for exploring West Cork, and the promise of the restaurant to return to after a day's touring is delectable.

● **OPEN:**
all year
● **AVERAGE PRICE:**
B&B low season £30-£45, mid season £40-£50
high season £45-£60 per person sharing

● **NOTES:**
Restaurant open Tue-Sat (Mon during Jul & Aug),
Dinner £29.
Restaurant closes end Oct-mid Mar
Children – high chair, cot
● 1.5 miles outside the village of Durrus on the Barleycove/Mizen Head road. Look for the blue gates on the right hand side of the road.

BOW HALL
Dick and Barbara Vickery
Castletownshend
Co Cork
Tel: (028) 36114

You meet Barbara Vickery, bow-tie bright, with those kind, kiddy-absorbing eyes, a little bundle of thoughtfulness and concern, and you think to yourself: why did we only book Bow Hall three days! I don't want to leave!

There are only three bedrooms in this fabulous house, and of course they all have names: the Apricot Room, the Toffee Room and the Oak Apple Room. The style mixes Shaker with a nod to the Arts & Crafts school, and it is an intensely family home: lots of wedding portraits and family snaps lining the walls, some nifty Oscar Peterson buzzing away in the background, a sitting room and library which looks like it has just walked out of a Frank Capra movie. Super cosy.

Mrs Vickery's breakfast muffins are already quietly famous, and one soft sweet mouthful will explain just why. She also makes a dynamite sausage, and light pancakes drizzled with maple syrup, and she cuddles your kid whilst you eat and chat to the other guests.

And at some epiphanous moment, you will say to yourself: "Why, this is just like a kiddies' book story, and I am in it!" And so you are, so you are.

● **OPEN:**
All year, except Xmas
● **ROOMS:**
Three rooms
All with private baths
● **AVERAGE PRICE:**
B&B £35 per person sharing
£5 single supplement

● **NOTES:**
No Credit Cards accepted
Dinner 8pm, £20, communal table
No Wheelchair Access
Enclosed Car Parking
Children – welcome, high chair, cot
● In Castletownshend village centre, on the right hand side as you drive down towards the sea.

CORTHNA LODGE
Loretta & Herbert Strickner
Schull, Co Cork
Tel: (028) 28517 Fax: 28032

Loretta Strickner's Corthna Lodge is a house where guests are destined to be thoroughly cared for. The evident care in the design of the rooms in this modern house, with their pastelly comfort and well-mannered charm, makes them cosy and comfortable, especially so when the wind is whipping about outside, as soon as summer fades and autumn begins.

Above all, it's a house where the owners take nothing for granted, but are always checking to see that things are just right, that you are as happy as they can manage to make you. More of this? More of that?, they ask.

The gentleness and sweetness of Loretta and Herbert Strickner themselves, and the attentive, tippy-toe air which they give to the house compounds the pleasure of being here, as do the delicious breakfasts – steaming coffee, fresh eggs and bread, handmade cheese from Gubbeen farm just down the hill.

"When the bad weather hit Schull, Loretta gave us electric under-blankets, switched on her central heating and lighted enormous fires in her sitting-room and brought us elevenses as we waited for the weather to clear", wrote one correspondent.

And you think, yes, that's just what Loretta would do.

● **OPEN:**
Easter-Oct
● **ROOMS:**
Six rooms, all en suite
● **AVERAGE PRICE:**
B&B £25 per person sharing
£30 single room

● **NOTES:**
No Dinner (good restaurants locally)
Wheelchair Access
Enclosed Car Parking
Children – welcome, high chair, cot, babysitting
● Just three minutes drive from the village of Schull. Go through the village towards Mizen Head, turn left up the hill, and then follow the signposts.

FORTVIEW HOUSE ⊙

Mrs Violet Connell
Gurtyowen, Toormore, Goleen, West Cork
Tel: (028) 35324
Fax: 35324

The only one problem with Violet Connell's lovely Fortview House is that once you stay here, you don't want to leave.

All of the elemental and dazzling charms of the Schull peninsula could be beckoning to you to get outside, to make hay with the day, but you just want to linger a little longer over breakfast — compote of fresh oranges and marmalade; homemade nut and grain muesli; homemade pancakes and maple syrup; hot potato cakes with crème fraîche and smoked salmon; local farmhouse cheese plate; a scramble of the eggs laid by their own happy, lazy hens; warm scones, hot coffee, fresh vegetable and fruit juices. And maybe as you are exploring the peninsula, you find yourself thinking about dinner: a little aperitif they make each evening to kick things off, then some good soup with brown bread. Then maybe a roast breast of duck, or an escalope of beef which will have been reared on the farm itself and which comes with a green pepper sauce, or maybe a t-bone steak from the same source. Then some local cheeses, as you finish the red wine. And a home-made pudding.

The only solution is to book for an extended stay.

● **OPEN:**
1 Mar-1 Nov
● **ROOMS:**
Five rooms
All en suite
● **AVERAGE PRICE:**
B&B £20-£25 per person sharing
£6.50 single supplement

● **NOTES:**
Dinner 8pm, £15, communal table
No Wheelchair Access
Enclosed Car Parking
Children — over 6yrs welcome
● Signposted 2km from Toormore on the main Durrus road (R591). 12km from Durrus, 9km from Goleen and Schull

10 GREAT BREAKFASTS

①
ANGLESEA TOWNHOUSE
DUBLIN, CO DUBLIN

②
ADÈLE'S
SCHULL, CO CORK

③
BALLYCORMAC HOUSE
BORRISOKANE, CO TIPPERARY

④
BUGGY'S GLENCAIRN INN
GLENCAIRN, CO WATERFORD

⑤
FORTVIEW HOUSE
GOLEEN, CO CORK

⑥
HANORA'S COTTAGE
CLONMEL, CO WATERFORD

⑦
HILTON PARK
CLONES, CO MONAGHAN

⑧
LACKEN HOUSE
KILKENNY, CO KILKENNY

⑨
MADDYBENNY FARMHOUSE
PORTRUSH, CO ANTRIM

⑩
THE OLD WORKHOUSE
DUNSHAUGLIN, CO MEATH

GARNISH HOUSE
Con & Hansi Lucey
Western Road, Cork City, Co Cork
Tel: (021) 275111 Fax: 273872
e-mail: garnish@iol.ie

The Esperanto of the People Business leaps into orbit on the Western Road. There is the promise, on a bright neon sign, of 'H & C, C.H., All Rooms', to tempt you, or 'B&B, Hot & Cold, Central Heating & Tea Making Facilities'. Which bit, you might ask, is it that runs hot and cold?

If all this shorthand sounds like so much Greek, then an evening in Hansi Lucey's Garnish House will have you composing your own Esperanto to Mrs Lucey's accomplishment of skills. 'Hospitality not Optional. Hot Never Cold. Charm Permanently on Tap. Endless Solicitude'.

Mrs Lucey was a nursing sister, and it is this she associates as her gift in the people business, though such decent friendliness is something instinctive, not something that can be learned.

'How are you? Did you sleep well? Were you comfortable? Would you like some more hot toast – it's on its way'.

On and on it goes, this wonderful litany of welcomes and solicitations, more important than any volume of promised, abbreviated, services. The rooms in Garnish House are naturally cosy and contain all you might want, but it is the spontaneity that makes Garnish such a fun place to be.

● **OPEN:**
All year
● **ROOMS:**
Fourteen rooms
All en suite
● **AVERAGE PRICE:**
B&B £25 per person sharing
£5 single supplement

● **NOTES:**
No Dinner (many local restaurants)
Wheelchair Access
Enclosed Car Parking
Children – welcome, high chair, cot, babysitting
● Five minutes walk from city centre, just opposite UCC.

LARCHWOOD HOUSE
Sheila & Aidan Vaughan
Pearson's Bridge
nr Ballylickey,
Co Cork
Tel: (027) 66181

Describing Larchwood House as a 'Restaurant With Rooms' is only partly correct.

There is a restaurant, of course, and upstairs there are four rooms, all of them en suite. But the truth of the matter is that Larchwood is, first and foremost, a family home, albeit a family home which just happens to have a restaurant, and happens to have four rooms upstairs for guests. The lounge is, for example, also the sitting room, whilst the dining room is simply a larger than usual family dining room, with various tables arrayed around the walls, some with a splendid view of the splendid garden.

And yet, if the designation 'Restaurant With Rooms' suggests a professional organisation, then Larchwood can certainly be described in this way. Sheila Vaughan is an expert cook, and an ambitious one.

Dinners are long and large, and there is a small wine list to choose from. So if the thought of only having to climb upstairs to bed sounds like just the sort of intensive relaxation you feel you need, then Larchwood, in its own way, is an unorthodox success.

● **OPEN:**
All year
● **ROOMS:**
Four rooms, all en suite
● **AVERAGE PRICE:**
B&B £25 per person

● **NOTES:**
Dinner 7pm-10pm, £24
No Wheelchair Access
Enclosed Car Parking
Children – over 6yrs welcome
● Turn off the N71 at Ballylickey and take the Kealkil Road for approximately 2 miles.
At Pearson's Bridge, take a sharp right.
The house is 300 yds on the right.

LETTERCOLLUM HOUSE
Con McLoughlin & Karen Austin
Timoleague, Co Cork
Tel: (023) 46251 Fax: 46270
e-mail: conmc@iol.ie
website: www.clon.ie/letterco.html

The last time we were enjoying Sunday lunch in
Lettercollum – one of the best bargains you can enjoy in
Ireland – a couple from Cork were having lunch with
their boys at the next table.

"We just had to get out of the city, just had to get away
for the night", they explained, and one could see how
Lettercollum House would be the perfect refuge for
stressed-out modern families.

The rooms are simple, but big and capacious. The cooking, by Con and Karen, is thrillingly flavourful, and the
house itself is a pure stress-free zone, a little oasis just
outside the lovely village of Timoleague.

It has a long history having been built in 1861, and its
various owners have included the Sisters of Mercy, which
means there are fine stained glass windows in what is
now the restaurant and was formerly a chapel.

Over the last year, the rooms have been upgraded, making them more comfortable, but no less suitable for families. There is a kitchen where you can feed the babies, and
a calm sitting room. And, then, at end of day, with the
babies asleep upstairs, there is wonderful cooking to
complete the pleasure equation of this smashing place.

● **OPEN:**
Open Mar-Dec (open off season for groups)
● **ROOMS:**
Nine rooms, all en suite, incl large family rooms
● **AVERAGE PRICE:**
B&B £18-£24 low season, £30 high season, per person
sharing

● **NOTES:**
Dinner £21.50
No Wheelchair Access
Enclosed Car Parking
Children – welcome, resident's kitchen, high chair, cot
● Lettercollum House is signposted from the first road
on the right coming out of Timoleague, heading towards
Clonakilty.

LISS ARD LAKE LODGE ⊙
Veith Turske & Claudia Turske
Skibbereen, Co Cork
Tel: (028) 22365
Fax: 40001
e-mail: lissardlakelodge@tinet.ie

Unlike other country house hotels, which are collated and furnished higgledy-piggledy, this glorious manor house enjoys an integrity and organic composition which is quite inspiring.

Partly this comes from the brave plainness of the style. The only decorations on the walls are mounted samples of the 249 varieties of butterfly which have been discovered in the 30-acre grounds. Otherwise, an interplay of colours is used to create contrast and a sense of space, and the plainness means that the rooms are terrifically calm. The style represents nothing less than an attempt at creating a perfect space, a perfect place.

The owners quote Thoreau in their brochure – "I love nature partly because she is not man, but a retreat from him... He makes me wish for another world. She makes me content with this". You could use Liss Ard as a retreat from clamouring society, and it is difficult to think of another place which would be so suitable. But the quote from Thoreau is apposite, in the case of Liss Ard, because here is a house that seems marvellously in union with its surroundings, which seems to have evolved out of the sense of organic wholeness which we find in the natural world.

● **OPEN:**
All year (except four weeks Jan/Feb)
● **ROOMS:**
Ten rooms, all en suite
● **AVERAGE PRICE:**
B&B £139 high season, £119 low season per person, including dinner

● **NOTES:**
Dinner 7pm-10pm, separate tables
No Wheelchair Access
Enclosed and Locked Car Parking
Children – welcome, high chair, cot, babysitting
● From Skibbereen take the road to Castletownshend and the house is signposted just outside the town.

LONGUEVILLE HOUSE ✪
The O'Callaghan family
Mallow
Co Cork
Tel: (022) 47156
Fax: 47459
e-mail: longueville_house_eire@msm.com

Hospitality is instinctive for the O'Callaghan family. What they have, they share. Their lovely old house. Their generous natures. Their exquisite food. As this story shows.

One day, in the ever-ongoing course of research, we accompanied William O'Callaghan on a visit to some of his interesting local suppliers. After the mushroom growers, we visited a fruit farm, where the owner also presented us with a couple of combs of honey. Back in Longueville, William told his mother, Jane, that he had been given a gift of the honey. "Wonderful!", she said. "We'll put it out in the morning for the guests' breakfast, that's the best honey you can get!".

Allied to this generosity is a degree of self-sufficiency which is dauntingly impressive. It is their own lamb which turns up on the plate, and most of the vegetables you will enjoy have come from no further than their own gardens. Salmon will have been hoisted from the Blackwater river. A small collation of wine is made every year, using the Muller-Thurgau grape.

This is a fine and important thing, for Mr O'Callaghan is one of the finest cooks in the country, the man who has made Longueville into a gastronomic temple.

● **OPEN:**
early Feb-20 Dec
● **ROOMS:**
Twenty rooms, all en suite
● **AVERAGE PRICE:**
B&B from £55-£82 per person sharing
single supplement £20-£40

● **NOTES:**
Dinner 8.15pm-9.15pm £30
No Wheelchair Access
Enclosed and Locked Car Parking
Children – welcome, high chair, cot, baby-listening
● Longueville House is 4 miles west of Mallow on the N72 to Killarney

MARIA'S SCHOOLHOUSE
Maria Hoare
Cahergal, Union Hall, Co Cork
Tel: (028) 33002/33062 Fax: 33002

The characters who operate the Schoolhouse, especially Maria Hoare herself and Francine, who does a lot of the cooking, are as full of joie de vivre as the Matisse jazz prints used throughout as decoration, and they give a timeless sense of youth to the whole place.

It is a very real place, the Schoolhouse: no artifice, no nonsense, just a happy collection of folk making happy food and creating a happy space. Whatever you do, don't miss the special breakfast where a slice of baked French toast is slathered with cream cheese and served with a fresh peach purée.

Dinners, meanwhile, specialise in vegetarian dishes, but whatever they cook – a gratin of French beans; roast spuds with a rosemary butter; creamed spinach; chicken breast filled with a tarragon cream cheese then wrapped in filo – will be drop-dead delicious.

Right throughout the schoolhouse, there is a bold use of colour in every room, not just on the walls and thanks to the various prints, but also with the eclectic collection of bedspreads. This is a place where each space has been carefully considered and then carefully achieved, but more by virtue of thoughtfulness than easy recourse to wads of cash.

● **OPEN:**
Mid Mar-early Jan
● **ROOMS:**
Eight rooms, all en suite
● **AVERAGE PRICE:**
B&B £19.50 per person sharing
£5 single supplement

● **NOTES:**
Dinner 7pm Mon-Sat, £12, Communal tables
Full Wheelchair Access
Enclosed Car Parking
Children – welcome, high chair, cot, babysitting
● Follow signs for Union Hall, then for Reen Pier and Maria's Schoolhouse, 1 mile from the village, the Schoolhouse is on your right, before you reach Reen Pier.

THE OLD BANK HOUSE
Marie & Michael Reise
Kinsale, Co Cork
Tel: (021) 774075/772968
Fax: 774296

The Old Bank House, a handsome, town-centre B&B in the ever-popular resort town of Kinsale, occupies a building that was, once upon a time, an old bank house, specifically the Munster and Leinster Bank.

It has retained something of the quiet, dignified calm of a bank, however, and its peacefulness can prove to be an oasis of cool sanity, somewhere that seems especially valuable during holiday times, when Kinsale can appear to be on the brink of overheating, almost on an hourly basis. First time visitors should know that this can be a hectic spot at holiday weekends, and anyone looking for a quiet time should maybe look elsewhere.

The trappings of the modern age are all here – direct dial telephones, multi-channel TV, big, elegant bathrooms – but Michael and Marie Reise never allow the house to sink into formulaic blandness, and they strive annually for changes and for improvements, features which will make the house more complete, more composed. The professionalism of the Reises – they formerly ran a restaurant in Kinsale before switching their talents to manning the Old Bank House – is almost a guarantee of good, care-free, relaxing times.

● **OPEN:**
All year, except Xmas
● **ROOMS:**
Nine rooms, all en suite
● **AVERAGE PRICE:**
B&B £35-£65 per person sharing
Single occupancy of double room £45-£70

● **NOTES:**
No Dinner (many restaurants locally)
No Wheelchair Access
No private parking
Children – welcome, but parents advised house not particularly suitable for toddlers
● Situated in the town centre, between the Supervalu and the Post Office.

SCILLY HOUSE INN
Karin Young & Bill Skelly
Scilly, Kinsale, Co Cork
Tel: (021) 772413
Fax: 774629

It is very easy indeed, if one has a mind to build or develop a luxury B&B, to simply throw money in the direction of your idea and to hope, finally, that a shower of cash will buy you the sort of good taste which discriminating guests will seek out.

Easy, but almost certainly doomed to failure. To create a luxury B&B needs, firstly, a sense of the place and importance of beauty, and the ability to make this beauty both tactile and, vitally, accessible.

Scilly House, a short walk from Kinsale and perched peering across the harbour, is a place that solves these problems, seemingly effortlessly.

The rooms are vast, and vastly comfortable, though nothing is ever overstated: colours are chosen as much for their ability to play with light and space and to accommodate the rafts of bright light which come hurling through the windows, bouncing back from the sea. Downstairs there is, again, subtlety and understatement, things left to speak for themselves. Whether you arrive with wishes of waterborne romance, or prefer to keep your feet firmly on the ground or thereabouts, this is a romantic house, its attractions always evident.

● **OPEN:**
beginning May-Oct
● **ROOMS:**
Seven rooms
All en suite
● **AVERAGE PRICE:**
B&B £45-£60 per person

● **NOTES:**
No Dinner (numerous local restaurants)
No Wheelchair Access
Enclosed and Locked Car Parking
Children – over 10yrs welcome
● Scilly House is just outside the centre of Kinsale, around the corner from the Man Friday restaurant, opposite the Spaniard pub.

SEA COURT
David Elder
Butlerstown, Bandon, Co Cork
Tel: (023) 40151 (Caretaker Tel: 023 40218)

Soft light, soft sea breezes, soft accents from the locals: the area around Butlerstown has a marshmallowy gentleness to it, a pastel impressionism which, on warm summer days as you wend and wind around the softly inclined roads, lends a certain light headedness to how one sees this quiet part of County Cork.

The gentleness continues if one stays at Sea Court. Though the front of this fine mansion is, incongruously, faced with slates, inside one finds a house which is respectfully shy, colourfully oblique, a place with the confidence of a long history.

David Elder lives here for part of the year, during which time he works diligently to restore the house, and allows himself the diversion of guests during the season. Mr Elder, naturally, is likewise soft-spoken and gentle-gestured, the perfect host for this warm, gracious, unimposing country house.

David Elder's restorations are carefully picked out in Wedgewood blues, fudgey terracotta, a cheeky Papal purple, colours which soak up the light and, in the big, breezy bedrooms, create the impression of hugely generous space. Furnishings are happily sparse – no nonsensical Victorian clutter destroys the lines of the rooms, hallways and landings – and the total effect is nothing less than uplifting.

● **OPEN:**
10 Jun-20 Aug
● **ROOMS:**
Six rooms. All en suite, or with private bath
● **AVERAGE PRICE:**
B&B £23.50 per person. Single supplement £5.50

● **NOTES:**
No Credit Cards accepted
Dinner 8pm, £17.50
No Wheelchair Access. Enclosed Car Parking
Children – welcome, high chair, cot, babysitting
● From Timoleague, cross the bridge, then turn left in front of the Abbey. Travel just over 2 miles, and you will see their sign.

SEA VIEW HOUSE HOTEL
Kathleen O'Sullivan
Ballylickey, Co Cork
Tel: (027) 50073
Fax: 51555

In Kathleen O'Sullivan's hotel, they do things right, simply from an instinct for good manners and care. That sentiment, that instinct, underlies everything that happens here, making it a special hotel.

The attention and kindness of the staff makes Sea View charming. They disarm your criticism of the decor, which makes no effort to co-ordinate from one room to another and which can often throw together too much clutter in the bedrooms.

The food they bring to the table, both at breakfast and, especially, at dinner, is so delicious, so buttery and creamy, that you forget your concern for artery and waistline: never mind comfort food, these dishes transport you all the way back to the womb.

People come here to have a good time, to celebrate the special events and days of their lives, and they do so with gusto, with determination to wring the best possible memories from the day that is in it. "I thought they were going to give me a big hug when I walked into the reception", a friend said of Sea View and, if you did indeed get a big hug when you walked into reception, well it wouldn't seem out of order.

● **OPEN:**
Mid Mar-mid Nov
● **ROOMS:**
Seventeen rooms
All en suite
● **AVERAGE PRICE:**
B&B £40-£45 per person sharing
£5 single supplement

● **NOTES:**
Dinner 7pm-9pm, £23-£25
Full Wheelchair Access
Car Parking
Children – welcome, high chair, cot, babysitting by arrangement
● From Bantry take road for Glengarriff. Hotel is 3 miles along this road on right, large notice at gate.

SEVEN NORTH MALL
Angela Hegarty
7 North Mall, Cork
Tel: (021) 397191
Fax: 300811

Some of the houses we feature in the Bridgestone guides quickly acquire cult status, and Angela Hegarty's townhouse, down towards the end of the river malls in Cork city, is one of those houses.

Aside from business folk, who can't tolerate the blandness of hotels, and travellers who revel in the house as a perfect place to stay in Cork city, you might just pass a diplomat on the stairs, or take breakfast with an ambassador. That's the sort of reputation 7 North Mall has acquired.

How has Mrs Hegarty done it? Well, if God is in the detail, then she is on chatting terms with the man. 7 North Mall is valuable because of the cool, understated air it possesses. The air of understatement is seen in the appreciation of the importance of carefully chosen furnishings, carefully chosen utensils, carefully chosen addendums. Mrs Hegarty's family is liberally sprinkled with architects, and it shows in the ever-careful consideration of each detail of this house.

No detail is too small to merit attention, and the care and enjoyment of furnishings and styles in 7 North Mall is inspiring. This attention to detail is important, for it makes the house both serene and relaxing.

● **OPEN:**
All year, except Xmas
● **ROOMS:**
Seven rooms
All en suite
● **AVERAGE PRICE:**
B&B £25-£30 per person sharing
£10 single supplement

● **NOTES:**
No Dinner (numerous local restaurants)
Wheelchair Access
Locked Car Parking
Children – over 12 years welcome
● Cork city centre, on the north bank of the north channel of the River Lee.

THE WEST CORK HOTEL
John Murphy
Ilen Street, Skibbereen
Co Cork
Tel: (028) 21277
Fax: 22333

The West Cork Hotel has long been something of a legend in West Cork, its fine, buttercup-yellow edifice a beacon which promised good food, good hospitality, above all a relaxed and generous way of doing things.

John Murphy continues the inimitable family traditions of the West Cork Hotel. A confident host, and a most amusing man, he is someone blessed with that hotelier's eye for seeing that things are done just right, just so.

The West Cork Hotel has been consistently innovative with its cooking, steadily progressive in terms of updating decor and upgrading specifications, but it has always clung to the atmosphere of family and familiarity which makes it someplace special.

It's not unusual, for example, to see three or four generations of a family altogether at dinner in the dining room here, and to learn that they have been coming at the same time, each year, for year after year after year. And it is not just visitors who flock back to the West Cork: locals treasure it for its affordability and its accessibility.

People find the West Cork to be a home from home, a place of relaxation, where things are properly done according to ageless standards of service.

● **OPEN:**
All year, except Xmas
● **ROOMS:**
Thirty six rooms, all en suite
● **AVERAGE PRICE:**
B&B £27.50-£39 per person sharing
£33-£39 single

● **NOTES:**
Dinner 6pm-9.30pm Mon-Sun, £19.50
No Wheelchair Access
Enclosed Car Parking
Children – welcome, high chair, cot
● Follow the N71 in the one way system out of Skibbereen, heading towards the West and the hotel is just before the Kennedy bridge as you leave town.

ARDNAMONA HOUSE & GARDENS

Amabel & Kieran Clarke
Lough Eske, Donegal, Co Donegal
Tel: (073) 22650 Fax: 22819
e-mail: ardnamon@tempoweb.com
website: http://www.tempoweb.com/ardnamon

Nowhere, but nowhere, can compare to the beauty of Lough Eske. This is an impossibly beautiful place. Walk down the stairs in Ardnamona in the morning, stroll to the front windows and the perfection of nature which you will see before you seems all too good to be true. The stillness, the concentrated surfeit of water and wood as the Blue Stack mountains cradle the eager waters of Lough Eske, is unforgettable.

Amabel and Kieran Clarke's house sits fast in the wrap of lough and forest, and the bloom of rich summer greens and blues is matched by the shocking russet vividness of the ferns in the winter. There are five rooms in the house, south facing, brightly pastelly, their modest design perfectly judged and effected. Mrs Clarke is a confident cook, which means that her food is simple – roast quail on toast, good roasted lamb, splendid gratins of courgette and other seasonal vegetables, excellent potatoes – the perfect dinner in the perfect house.

In the hands of anybody else, Ardnamona might well wind up like some sort of stuffed architectural and botanical peacock, but Kieran and Amabel puncture any sort of stuffiness with their calm, democratic spirits. A glorious place.

● **OPEN:**
15 Mar-31 Oct
● **ROOMS:**
Five rooms, three en-suite
● **AVERAGE PRICE:**
B&B £35-£45 per person sharing, £10 single supplement

● **NOTES:**
Dinner 8.30pm, £18, communal table
Enclosed car parking
No Wheelchair Access
Children – welcome, high chair, cot, babysitting
● Leave Donegal on N15 towards Letterkenny. After 5kms take small turning on left marked Harvey's Point. Keep straight for 7kms, entrance is on right.

CASTLE MURRAY HOUSE
Thierry Delcros & Claire Seguin
Dunkineely, Co Donegal
Tel: (073) 37022 Fax: 37330

Castlemurray's somewhat grand name is something of a red herring, for this is not a House as it is commonly understood in Ireland, but is instead that glorious French concept of the Restaurant with Rooms.

No one else in Ireland, however, seems able to make the idea work just so well as Claire and Thierry Delcros. Partly, perhaps, this is because they are born to it and whilst their delightful French accents are now deliciously peppered with Donegalese, the Delcros work in a fashion that is nothing other than French in orientation and organisation.

You could come here with nothing more in mind than to feast your eyes on Thierry's superb food, perhaps the best cooking in Donegal, but if you can drag your gaze away from the plate, then the house offers some of the most astonishingly gorgeous views you will find anywhere in the country.

In wintertime the light dies slowly, leaving a smudge of spectral light on top of the hills which is echoed by the lapping fringe of the waves. In summer the golds and blues are mesmerising, always changing. The gentleness of the house is doubly comfortable in the midst of the relentlessness of Donegal.

● **OPEN:**
All year (closed Mon-Wed off season)
● **ROOMS:**
Ten rooms, all en suite
● **AVERAGE PRICE:**
B&B £30 per person sharing
£24-£28 single

● **NOTES:**
Dinner 7pm-9.30pm, from £28, separate tables (Sun dinner 3pm-8pm)
Wheelchair Access
Enclosed and Locked Car Parking
Children — welcome, high chair, cot, babysitting
● Castlemurray is signposted just after the village of Dunkineely, on the N56 road west from Donegal to Bruckless and Killybegs.

CROAGHROSS COTTAGE

John & Kay Deane
Portsalon, Letterkenny
Co Donegal
Tel: (074) 59548
Fax: 59548
e-mail: jkdeane@iol.ie

The strand at Portsalon is a gorgeous two mile curve of fine white sand, which beckons to you as you look down on it from the elevated vantage of John and Kay Deane's Croaghross Cottage. Come on!, it says. Come on!

So off you go, suddenly rendered inhumanly diminutive by the grandness and the gloriousness of the ever-changing skies and the crash of the water.

And, four exhilarating, miles later, you find yourself back in Croaghross, enjoying Kay's country cooking – lovely egg and prawn mousse, some fillet of pork with roasted peaches and champ, crisp broccoli, nice old-style celery in a white sauce, some apple and blackberry tart with vanilla ice cream – and maybe, just maybe, those eyelids will begin to flutter and begin to droop, and you will stumble off to bed, to sleep the sleep of the just.

"We certainly notice it when people are here for the first night, and they have been out golfing or walking", says John Deane as he pours you a belt of gin'n'tonic before dinner. "The fresh air really has an effect on them!". Croaghross is therapeutic, and the hospitality of the Deanes is efficient, understated, effective. They do things right.

● **OPEN:**
17 Mar-30 Sep
● **ROOMS:**
Five rooms, all en suite
● **AVERAGE PRICE:**
B&B £15-£25 per person sharing
£5 single supplement

● **NOTES:**
Dinner 7.30pm-8pm, £15, separate tables
Full Wheelchair Access
Private Parking beside house
Children – welcome, high chair, cot, babysitting
● Turn right at the crossroads in Portsalon, and after half a mile, opposite golf club, turn left at signpost.

ANGLESEA TOWN HOUSE

Helen Kirrane
63 Anglesea Road, Ballsbridge, Dublin 4
Tel: (01) 668 3877
Fax: 668 3461

We have continuous discussions, during the course of the year as the Bridgestone guides are being researched and written, on just who serves the finest breakfast in the country.

There are many contenders, often for many different reasons. Some will offer terrific breads, or handmade butter, and others will have porridge with whiskey, or fresh fish to be pan fried. Some will have amazing coffee, or perhaps beautiful tableware. Some might just offer the best smoked bacon you can get your hands on, or the silkiest scrambled eggs.

But, whatever and wherever we discuss, Helen Kirrane's house is always up there at the top of the list. For there is no breakfast quite like the Anglesea breakfast, no other procedure so orchestrated and meticulous, so ornate and comprehensive. It is gargantuan, and quite gorgeous, a re-definition of what breakfast can be.

It begins with their own cereals, whether fine muesli or rich porridge, progresses on through fresh seasonal fruits, into lush omelettes stuffed with smoked salmon, scrambled eggs or perhaps devilled kidneys or a terrific kedgeree, with chocolate pastries to end (!) and lakes of coffee and mountains of fresh bread all around. It is an incredible experience, nothing less.

● **OPEN:**
6 Jan-22 Dec
● **ROOMS:**
Seven rooms, all en-suite
● **AVERAGE PRICE:**
B&B £45 per person

● **NOTES:**
No Dinner (plenty of local restaurants)
Enclosed car parking
No Wheelchair Access
Children – welcome, cots, babysitting
● From Jury's Hotel in Ballsbridge, cross the river, take first right onto Anglesea Road. The house is signposted on Anglesea Road.

CHESTNUT LODGE ⊙

Nancy Malone
2 Vesey Place, Monkstown, Co Dublin
Tel: (01) 280 7860
Fax: 280 1466

Nancy Malone's house is one of the cult addresses in Ireland. Beautiful, high-ceilinged, the cream in the crop of a Georgian terrace, it is a svelte, consoling, uplifting place, and its location, in the quiet embrace of a quiet Monkstown road, near to the ferry at Dun Laoghaire, close to town but far enough away to give one a flavour of the villages of Dublin, merely adds to its splendour.

If its aspect is just right, it is further congratulated in the attention to small details which Nancy and her daughters ensure are correctly in place. The house is beautifully understated in design terms, just as it should be. There is nothing gaudy, nothing overdone. Grandness is bestowed by the scale of the house, and Ms Malone otherwise leaves well alone.

Breakfast is a timeless joy: fine silver teapots and glistening cutlery, nutty soda bread and fresh orange juice, delicious compotes and muesli which are one of Ms Malone's specialities, beautifully scrambled eggs with bacon, fine linen. The fact that such care is taken over everything gives great pleasure. Making sure everything is done properly is one of the things that Nancy does properly in Chestnut Lodge. A delight.

● **OPEN:**
All year, except Xmas
● **ROOMS:**
Four rooms, all en suite
● **AVERAGE PRICE:**
B&B £32.50 per person sharing
£35-£40 single

● **NOTES:**
No Dinner
No Wheelchair Access
No private parking
Children – welcome, high chair, cot
● Coming from central Dublin, pass Monkstown Church, take the next turn right onto Sloperton Road. The first terrace is De Vesci terrace off Sloperton, the second is Vesey Place, facing an open park.

10 HOUSES NEAR THE MAJOR ROADS, AIRPORTS & FERRIES

1
BALLYTEIGUE HOUSE
CHARLEVILLE, CO LIMERICK (SHANNON AIRPORT)

2
CHESTNUT LODGE
MONKSTOWN, CO DUBLIN (DUN LAOGHAIRE FERRY)

3
ECHO LODGE
BALLINGARRY, CO LIMERICK (SHANNON AIRPORT)

4
FURZIESTOWN
TACUMSHANE, CO WEXFORD (ROSSLARE FERRY)

5
GARNISH HOUSE
CORK, CO CORK (CORK AIRPORT & FERRY)

6
McMENAMIN'S
WEXFORD, CO WEXFORD (ROSSLARE FERRY)

7
MOYTURA LODGE
DUBLIN, CO DUBLIN (DUN LAOGHAIRE PORT)

8
PRESTON HOUSE
ABBEYLEIX, CO LAOIS (N8)

9
SALVILLE HOUSE
ENNISCORTHY, CO WEXFORD (ROSSLARE FERRY)

10
7 NORTH MALL
CORK, CO CORK (CORK AIRPORT & FERRY)

THE CLARENCE ⊖
Claire O'Reilly
6-8 Wellington Quay, Dublin 2
Tel: (01) 670 9000 Fax: 670 7800
e-mail: clarence@indigo.ie
website: http://www.theclarence.ie

They were smart enough, the people whose job it was to design The Clarence, to realise that boutique hotels who sacrifice integrity at the altar of pure contemporary design, are destined to look outdated in about 2 years flat.

And so, with the sort of good taste and savvy one normally presumes wealthy people have little time for – the hotel is owned by Bono and The Edge of pop group U2 and Dublin businessman Harry Crosbie, none of whom are short the odd fortune – the design of the hotel has been achieved with boldness and more than a little brilliance.

The colours are strong, the use of wood in the bedrooms and public rooms perfectly judged, the ambition of creating pleasureful spaces by virtue of tactile furnishings terrifically well achieved. Other upmarket hotels which have come after The Clarence look like just so much compromise compared to this miracle of design, a place where good judgement has found a triumphal home.

Sure it's expensive, but it's worth it, for there is great pleasure to be enjoyed in this idyll of good taste. The restaurant of the hotel, The Tea Rooms, is sublime, and Michael Martin's food amongst the best in the city.

● **OPEN:**
All year
● **ROOMS:**
One Penthouse, Four suites, forty-four rooms, all en suite
● **AVERAGE PRICE:**
£175-£190 per room; £400-£535 per suite; £1,450 penthouse (all rates per night)

● **NOTES:**
Dinner 6.30pm-10.30pm, (Sun till 10pm) from £17.50
Full Wheelchair Access
Valet parking service (locked parking)
Children – welcome, high chair, cot, babysitting
● Overlooking the River Liffey.

THE HIBERNIAN HOTEL
David Butt
Eastmoreland Place, Ballsbridge, Dublin 4
Tel: (01) 668 7666
Fax: 660 2655
e-mail: info@hibernianhotel.ie
website:
http://www.slh.com/slh/pages/i/ianirea.html

The Hibernian doesn't feel like an hotel. It feels, instead, like a family home, where they just happen to take guests. Except nobody seems to be a guest, they seem to be family. Most everyone seems to be on first name terms – "Morning Eric. Morning Niall", you say first thing in the morning as you head in for breakfast, behaving as if you have known the staff all your life. And they, in turn, have your name in a flash, and remember it, when you next are back in The Hibernian. "How are you?", they ask, and they mean it.

It's a mighty ability, but it comes as no surprise, for David Butt is the general manager of the hotel, and he is one of the finest hoteliers you can meet: genial, expert, genuine, a man able to motivate staff to create a special atmosphere, to create a place where they seem to be able to read your mind. Indeed, when you turn off busy Baggot Street and then drive into the hotel, you seem to enter a little republic of calm and dignity.

In the kitchen, David Foley's cooking is memorable. And such, indeed, is The Hibernian: memorable.

● **OPEN:**
All year
● **ROOMS:**
Forty rooms, all en suite
● **AVERAGE PRICE:**
£145-£160 per room (suites from £180)
£110 per night single

● **NOTES:**
Dinner 6.30pm-10pm, (7pm-9pm Sun, residents only) from £21.95-£25.95
Full Wheelchair Access
Off street Parking
Children – welcome, high chair, cot
● Just off Upper Baggot Street, where it meets Pembroke road. Turn left at the drive-in AIB bank.

THE MORGAN

Paddy Shevlin
10 Fleet Street, Dublin 2
Tel: (01) 679 3939
Fax: 679 3946
e-mail: morganht@iol.ie

This ingenious little boutique hotel has a refreshing tactility about it, helped by the involvement of the artist Siobhan McDonald.

"The idea of working with one artist was our ambition to create pieces that work with the senses", they will tell you, but in truth the clever arrangement and furnishings of the rooms means that The Morgan itself is a sensual place, all told.

The walls of the rooms are decorated in neutral shades, to show the strong reds and navy blues of the chairs and carpets, with beech furniture perfectly accenting the colours. Cotton sheets and the straight, simple lines of the beds flesh out the tactile nature of the rooms, making them comfortable, comforting. Whilst all the modern telecommunication mod cons are also available, it is the ability of the rooms to be gracious and graceful which counts.

Breakfast comes to the room – the lobby is the only public area, until a second phase of the hotel is completed – in utensils which are a roll call of the modern design gurus: Starck, Aalto, Stelton, Alessi and others. Despite being almost in the heart of Temple Bar, the genius of The Morgan is its ability to feel like a hideaway.

● **OPEN:**
All year, except Xmas
● **ROOMS:**
Forty-three rooms, all en suite
● **AVERAGE PRICE:**
from £120 per room
£95 per night single

● **NOTES:**
All Sports Café serving dinner. Room service menu.
Full Wheelchair Access
Off street Parking, charged to guest
Children – welcome, high chair, cot
● In Temple Bar, on Fleet Street, across from the ESB shop.

MOYTURA HOUSE
Corinne & Alain Giacometti
Saval Park Road, Dalkey
Co Dublin
Tel: (01) 285 2371
Fax: 2350633
e-mail: giacomet@indigo.ie

An artistic spirit is evident in Moytura, a lovely Victorian house designed by John Loftus Robinson. When you talk to Corinne Giacometti, both about the style of this gracious place and about her cooking, you are confronted immediately by the importance of an individual aesthetic in her work, the necessity for her house to be tactile and pleasing, to be welcoming.

Perhaps it is because Mrs Giacometti trained as an interior architect that she so evidently succeeds in her ambitions, which means that the formal style of this house is tinged with a vital air of bohemianism, a sense of a freewheeling, free spirit, which comes from the assured decoration.

"I started to take guests because I thought I would enjoy it, and I did", she says, and the guests enjoy her excellent breakfasts – oeufs en cocote; fresh scones and bread; home-made muesli; seasonal fruits. The location of the house makes it a good first night-last night place if you are taking the ferry, and Dalkey itself is an ever-charming village. Mrs Giacometti also appreciates the need to be able to give guests lots of information and advice, so that one can get the very most out of the area.

● **OPEN:**
Mar-Oct
● **ROOMS:**
Three rooms, all en suite
● **AVERAGE PRICE:**
£35 per person sharing
£10 single supplement

● **NOTES:**
No Dinner
No Wheelchair Access
Unsuitable for young children
● Dalkey village is seven miles south of Dublin. Entering the village, turn right. Take the third road on the left, and Moytura is the corner house, first gate on the right.

NUMBER 31 ⊖

Brian & Mary Bennett
31 Leeson Close
Dublin 2
Tel: (01) 676 5011
Fax: 676 2929
e-mail: number31@iol.ie

This little mews house, set just back off the nightclub-strewn strip of Leeson Street, is unabashedly modernist, with a sunken seating area in the mosaic-clad living room that has the confidence of a classic.

It is a favourite Dublin place for many folk, who enjoy not only the style of the house, but also the friendly breakfast atmosphere – often too friendly, and impossible to drag yourself away from in order to get some work done! – and the communality which quickly builds between people staying here. The unselfconscious calm of No 31 arises from Brian and Mary's instinctive hospitality, and they make sure you are introduced to everyone, make sure you are brought up to date with what they are doing, and with all the new chat and gossip.

The Bennetts have now bought the principal house of the mews, on Fitzwilliam Place. The principal house, of course, is Georgian, so Number 31 now allows you the choice of staying slap-up to date in the twentieth century, or else regressing back to a time of great elegance. Many regular visitors find that they prefer the original house, however, so for a first visit it is worth trying to get into the Mews.

● **OPEN:**
All year, except 1 week at Xmas
● **ROOMS:**
Eighteen rooms, all en suite
● **AVERAGE PRICE:**
B&B £35-£47 per person sharing
£45-£70 single

● **NOTES:**
No Dinner (numerous local restaurants)
Limited Wheelchair Access
Locked Car Parking
Children – over 10 yrs welcome
● Turn at Cooper's Restaurant onto Leeson Close. First house on right is "No 8", second is No 31.

THE ARDAGH HOTEL
Stephane & Monique Bauvet
Ballyconeely Road, Clifden, Connemara,
Co Galway
Tel: (095) 21384 Fax: 21314
ardaghhotel@tinet.ie

Stephane and Monique Bauvet's Ardagh Hotel is an exception to the standard hotel rule, which says that beauty of location will almost certainly mean the owners won't feel they have to try in any other departments, seemingly believing that we can always eat the views.

In The Ardagh, where the location is quite heart-stoppingly lovely, we nevertheless find that the public rooms are comfortable, and so are the bedrooms – the rooms to chase after are those which overlook the bay – and the staff are helpful and personable.

But it is with Monique Bauvet's cooking that we see the Ardagh at its very best. Enjoyed in the upstairs restaurant with its stunning views out over Ardbear Bay, she will marinate Irish goat's cheese and then serve it with a salad dressed with Tio Pepe, or serve duck confit with cucumber and spring onions, but alongside these nouvellish touches there are classic starters such as poached chicken livers with a Cumberland sauce, seafood chowder, smoked salmon roulade with a river trout mousse.

Main courses once again show this mix of the daring and the formal, matching beef fillet with a Madagascar pepper sauce, or brill with roasted peppers, or a classic such as grilled sole with a chive and lemon butter. It's a cult, local favourite.

● **OPEN:**
End Mar-end Oct
● **ROOMS:**
Twenty-one rooms, all en suite
● **AVERAGE PRICE:**
B&B from £42.50 per person sharing
£15 single supplement

● **NOTES:**
Dinner 7.15pm-9.30pm, £27, separate tables
No Wheelchair Access
Enclosed Car Parking. Children – welcome, high chair, cot
● From Galway follow N59 to Clifden. Then follow sign to Ballyconeely (hotel also signposted).

BALLYNAHINCH CASTLE HOTEL
John O'Connor
Recess, Connemara, Co Galway
Tel: (095) 31006
Fax: 31085
e-mail: bhinch@iol.ie
website: http://commerce.ie/ballynachinch

All you have to do in Ballynahinch is to walk through the front door, plonk yourself in the big sofa in front of the fire, order a whiskey and soda, and bang! Baby, you are in Connemara.

Maharajah Ranjitsinji bought the house which is today Ballynahinch Castle, back in the 1930s, in order to entertain his friends during the winter. Today, the Castle Hotel, despite its title, still feels more like a country house than many of the country houses in Ireland.

It is relaxing and unpretentious, and staffed by young people who disport themselves likewise. For though it is big beamed like a castle, and grey like an hotel, Ballynahinch has never lost the principle of pleasure-pursuit which led to its being built, originally, as a weekend sporting retreat. The bedrooms which face the river are well worth the extra money, as these offer the best views and the most space, and are worth trying to reserve.

Many come here to fish on the skirling river, others to shoot woodcock, others for good-value winter weekends when the big fires, agreeable food and the do-nothing ambience of Ballynahinch find the place at its best, and the fine value-for-money is a big attraction.

● **OPEN:**
All year, except Xmas, 2 weeks in Feb
● **ROOMS:**
Twenty-eight rooms, All en suite
● **AVERAGE PRICE:**
B&B £48-£54 low season, £62-£72 high season, per person sharing, £20 single supplement

● **NOTES:**
Dinner 7pm-9pm, from £23, separate tables
No Wheelchair Access
Enclosed Car Parking
Children — welcome, high chair, cot, babysitting with prior notice
● Signposted from the N59 Galway/Clifden road.

ERRISEASK COUNTRY HOUSE HOTEL

Stefan & Christian Matz
Ballyconeely, Clifden
Connemara
Co Galway
Tel: (095) 23553 Fax: 23639

Maybe it is the contrast between the ferociously wild elements which can quickly whip up outside Erriseask – the hotel is pitched right beside the shore of Mannin Bay – and the calm interior, with its demure bar and seating area and formal dining room, which makes Erriseask such a welcoming tabernacle of good times.

Maybe, but what can be definitely stated about Stefan and Christian Matz's restaurant with rooms – perhaps a more accurate description of the complex – is that the former is a shy, front of house chap whilst his brother is one of the finest cooks working in Ireland at the present time. Put them together, along with the fine new apartments which look out over the sea, and you have an hypnotic alliance.

Stefan Matz's cooking is a mesmerising fusion of discipline and daring, and reciting the dishes doesn't even hint at the glories of taste they can achieve: freshly smoked terrine of wild duck on a bed of sautéed wild mushrooms; souffléd fillets of turbot in a warm sauce vinaigrette of fresh tomatoes; variation of magret of duck on a bed of home-made noodles; a soufflé of fromage blanc and oranges; white coffee ice cream with a dark chocolate mousse.

● **OPEN:**
End Mar-end Oct
● **ROOMS:**
Thirteen rooms, all en suite
● **AVERAGE PRICE:**
B&B £32.50-£48.50 per person sharing
£19 single supplement

● **NOTES:**
Dinner 6.30pm-9pm, £24-£34
Limited Wheelchair Access
Enclosed Car Parking
Children – one family bedroom, high chair, cot
● From Clifden follow signposts to Ballyconeely
(via Coast Road).

GARRAUNBAUN HOUSE
John & Catherine Finnegan
Moyard
Connemara, Co Galway
Tel: (095) 41649 Fax: 41649

Garraunbaun was built in 1852, and its design fuses early Victoriana with the fine stature of an imposing Georgian manor house. The rooms are statuesque, the bedrooms gigantic, with beds of orgiastic enormity – these really do have to be seen to be believed.

The views from the front windows reach out across the tranquillity of Lough Garraunbaun, Ballynakill Bay and to the Twelve Bens beyond, the sort of vista which makes one long to strap on the boots and get set to do some serious walking or some fine fishing.

But, should the rain hammer and the wind roar – as it is given to do in these parts – then here is a house where you want to tuckle up in front of the fire with a good book or a brainless magazine, and let the day dissolve into relaxed nothingness.

Delia Finnegan cooks in an astute style, which favours flavour over everything. Some good local wild smoked salmon, a fine fricassee with tasty chicken, good cheeses, scrummy puddings, and the wine list has some fine, rarely-seen clarets which are especially enjoyable. Garraunbaun is a house where you are quickly at your ease, and quickly locked in friendship with your fellow guests.

● **OPEN:**
All year
● **ROOMS:**
Four rooms, three en suite, 1 with private bathroom
● **AVERAGE PRICE:**
B&B £20-£30 per person sharing
Special rates off season and weekly board

● **NOTES:**
Dinner 8pm, £15 separate or communal tables
Wheelchair Access
Enclosed Car Parking
Children – high chair, cot, babysitting. video films
for all ages
● From Galway take the N59, following signs for
Clifden, then Cleggan. Then follow the Westport sign
and you will find Garraunbaun signs 3km further.

KILLEEN HOUSE
Catherine Doyle
Killeen, Bushypark
Galway
Tel: (091) 524179
Fax: 528065

Catherine Doyle's Killeen House is a fascinating place. A few miles out of Galway, it is immediately imposing as you drive up to its grand façade, dating from 1840.

But it is inside that the real fun starts. Ms Doyle used to work in the antiques business, and has managed to furnish each room in different, particular, design periods. As she says herself, "It would be impossible to do it today, because you could neither find, nor afford, the pieces".

Lucky for the traveller, then, that Catherine amassed her fine furnishings over the years, for it has allowed her to create a perfectly unique house.

The Art Deco room, for example, is a perfect piece of composition, with each element perfectly united in style with every other piece.

The effect in each of the suites – whether it be the Georgian, Victorian, Regency or Edwardian – is to create rooms which have absolutely no discordant design notes whatsoever, which makes them wonderfully inviting.

The public rooms are no less expert, and no less welcoming, and Ms Doyle has an aesthete's eye for every detail, including the hand-written breakfast menu. Killeen is also a great location for exploring both Galway city and Connemara.

● **OPEN:**
All year, except Xmas
● **ROOMS:**
Five rooms, all en suite
● **AVERAGE PRICE:**
B&B £35-£40 per person sharing
£15 single supplement

● **NOTES:**
No Dinner
No Wheelchair Access
Enclosed Car Parking
Children – over 12 yrs welcome
● Bushypark is situated between Galway and Moycullen on the N59, 4 miles from Galway city centre.

MOYCULLEN HOUSE
Philip & Marie Casburn
Moycullen, Co Galway
Tel: (091) 555566 Fax: 555566

Strategically situated, just after the wildness of Galway city, and just before the wilderness of Connemara, Moycullen offers familiarity and the assurance of fond memories each time you return to it.

An old sporting lodge built for wild west of Ireland week-ends, it is an altogether affable place. Architecturally it is a rarity in Ireland, set precisely in the Arts and Crafts style, a design which allows it to seem quaint yet proud, and which evokes visions of boozy country weekends spent huntin', shootin' and fishin'.

But it is Philip and Marie Casburn themselves who provide the core of Moycullen's soft focus, hazy and lazy air. Their easy ease, and Marie's unflustered comfort cooking, are as essential a part of Moycullen as the antique baths, the cushiony carpets, the cranky furniture, the buckets of fresh air.

Everything in the house, from the beds with their soft creakiness, to the gripping comfort of the chairs, to the succulence of mashed spuds with roast lamb preceded by kidneys in a sherry sauce and followed by a big creamy gateau, seems to knock the pent-up stuffing out of you, leaving you wanting more of this restfulness, and more of this graceful, naïve, house.

● **OPEN:**
Mar-Oct
● **ROOMS:**
Five rooms, one en suite, four with private bathrooms
● **AVERAGE PRICE:**
B&B £30-£35 per person sharing
£10 single supplement

● **NOTES:**
Dinner 7pm, £20 communal table
No Wheelchair Access
Enclosed Car Parking
Children – high chair, babysitting
● From Galway take the N59 (Clifden Road) to Moycullen village. Turn left in the village on to the Spiddal Road. The entrance to the house is 1.5km on left.

NORMAN VILLA ✪
Dee & Mark Keogh
86 Lower Salthill, Galway, Co Galway
Tel: (091) 521131 Fax: 521131

This gorgeous house captivates everyone who stays here, thanks to the ingenuity and beauty of its design, and thanks especially to the irrepressible hospitality of Mark and Dee Keogh.

More than almost any other address in Ireland, Norman Villa is a living, pulsing space, with the Keoghs endlessly rearranging, redecorating and redesigning in order to make it better and better.

They have a truly organic relationship with the house, their energy feeding its needs, keeping it up to scratch and beyond, which explains how they talk so easily about "Norman", as if the house had its own personality, its own heartbeat.

And, truth be told, it does. You return, year after year, and there is a new aspect of the house uncovered, some new piece of art causing you to look again at a particular room, some new piece of salvage or artefact beautifully restored and arranged with shocking cleverness and originality.

But its beauty would be nothing with the hospitality which is endlessly on tap here. Mark and Dee are endlessly fascinated and interested by their guests, and there is nothing going on in Galway that they do not know about. It all adds up to an exhilarating address.

● **OPEN:**
All year, including Xmas
● **ROOMS:**
Five rooms, all en suite
● **AVERAGE PRICE:**
B&B £30 per person sharing
£5 single supplement.
Surcharge on bank holidays and race week.

● **NOTES:**
No Dinner (except at Xmas)
No Wheelchair Access
Locked Car Parking
Children – over 6yrs welcome. 35% discount. Babysitting by arrangement.
● The house is beside PJ Flaherty's pub in lower Salthill.

QUAY HOUSE ✪
Paddy & Julia Foyle
Clifden, Connemara, Co Galway
Tel: (095) 21369
Fax: 21608
e-mail: thequay@iol.ie

He is, perhaps, the ultimate iconoclast, is Paddy Foyle.
You think he has created perfection in his houses and his restaurants, places of wondrous charm and comfort, and he will then take it apart and rebuild it and do it differently.

And you might wonder why, but then you realise that he saw his previous incarnation as only a step on the road to perfection, and you realise that once again he has inched forward, redefining, sharpening, perfecting his vision. He is a man unafraid to shatter what seems perfect. The ultimate iconoclast.

The Quay House now has 14 rooms, with seven rooms in the original house and seven new studio rooms in the adjoining building, each overlooking the harbour. Six of these new rooms have small kitchens, and are large enough – 550sq ft – for families, so anyone who wishes to do some self-catering will find them perfect.

The house sits down on the old harbour, far enough out of Clifden to escape it when it overheats, and it is a special place, which Paddy and Julia Foyle further decorate with their graciousness and wise experience. In the wildness of Connemara, it amounts to a magical place, a haven for those who love the unique.

● **OPEN:**
End Mar-end Oct (or by special arrangement)
● **ROOMS:**
Fourteen rooms, all en suite, some with fitted kitchens
● **AVERAGE PRICE:**
B&B £30-£45 per person sharing
£10 single supplement

● **NOTES:**
No dinner (local restaurants recommended)
Wheelchair Access
Enclosed Car Parking by arrangement only
Children – welcome, high chair, cot
● Three minutes by car from Clifden town centre, down on the harbour.

10 HOUSES FOR STYLE LOVERS

(1)
BUGGY'S GLENCAIRN INN
GLENCAIRN, CO WATERFORD

(2)
THE CLARENCE
DUBLIN, CO DUBLIN

(3)
ECHO LODGE
BALLINGARRY, CO LIMERICK

(4)
LISS ARD LAKE LODGE
SKIBBEREEN, CO CORK

(5)
THE MORGAN
DUBLIN, CO DUBLIN

(6)
No 31
DUBLIN, CO DUBLIN

(7)
NORMAN VILLA
GALWAY, CO GALWAY

(8)
THE QUAY HOUSE
CLIFDEN, CO GALWAY

(9)
7 NORTH MALL
CORK, CO CORK

(10)
SHELBURNE LODGE
KENMARE, CO KERRY

RADHARC AN CHLAIR
Mrs Bríd Poíl
Inis Oirr, Aran Islands
Co Galway
Tel: (099) 75019
Fax: 75019

"Stayed with Bríd Poíl in spring, and all is well", writes a friend. "More en suites as is the trend. Food and service as good as ever, with the food being more adventurous following a few new courses".

A nice, neat and nifty summary of Mrs Poíl's house, on Inis Oirr, the smallest of the three Aran Islands. Steady upgrading, steady culinary progression, but still with the firm dependables of friendliness and service to make your stay a delight.

Bríd Poíl may not be an Aran islander herself – she has the soft blue eyes and the sea-sand coloured hair of someone hailing from County Clare – but there is no better base from which to seek out the measure of little Inis Oirr than her smart bungalow in the village of Baile an Chaisleáin.

At dinner time you can expect the comforting odours of sweet lamb, fresh fish, fine floury spuds. What animates Mrs Poíl's cooking is not just her skill and her sheer love of food, but the fact that she has a student's eagerness to know more, and an enlivening appreciation and respect for food animates her work, all the way from soft, babbly soups to soporific, creamy cakes.

● **OPEN:**
All year
● **ROOMS:**
Six rooms, five en suite
● **AVERAGE PRICE:**
B&B £15-£16 per person sharing
£2 single supplement

● **NOTES:**
No Credit Cards accepted
Dinner 6.30pm, £11 separate tables
Bring Your Own Wine
No Wheelchair Access
Children – welcome, high chair, cot, babysitting
Peadar Poil always meets visitors who are pre-booked and gives you a lift up to the house (in his tractor)

THE CAPTAIN'S HOUSE
Jim & Mary Milhench
The Mall, Dingle
Co Kerry
Tel: (066) 51531 Fax: 51079
e-mail: captigh@tinet.ie

Jim Milhench was a sea captain, before he met Mary and they decided to crew together on the charming vessel which is The Captain's House, which explains how this landlocked place, smack in the centre of Dingle, gets its name.

It is a rather small house, but here the scale has been utilised in such a way that it creates an intimate, welcoming environment: it comes as no surprise to learn that many guests who return here request specific rooms, in particular room 10, the one with the sloping roof.

The cosiness of the rooms and the superb housekeeping make for a place which oozes comfort, and that comfort is then further congratulated by the splendour of the cooking and the baking — just don't pass on the porter cake, offered to all guests with tea when they arrive, for it is a rich, boozy, beautiful concoction.

Local knowledge brings in fuscia honey from Ballyferriter as one of the fine ingredients for breakfast, alongside baked ham and local goat's cheese, Mary's own muesli, an array of peaches and prunes and mandarins, and their own marmalade, buffeted by bumper egg dishes and the traditional fried Irish breakfast.

● **OPEN:**
Apr-Nov
● **ROOMS:**
Seven rooms, all en-suite
● **AVERAGE PRICE:**
B&B £22 per person sharing
£30 single room

● **NOTES:**
No Dinner
No private parking
No Wheelchair Access, No Children
● At the roundabout approaching Dingle town turn right, taking exit for town centre/Connor Pass and house is 200 mtrs on left and approached by footbridge over the Mall River.

CHURCHFIELD

Joêlle Kerihuel & Chris Johnson
Churchfield, Lispole
Co Kerry
Tel: (066) 51843 Fax: 51067
e-mail: joelle@empathy.iol.ie

"It's not a B&B, not a hotel, not a guest house – it's more a way of life", wrote one guest who stayed at Churchfield. It's a fine house, built originally by the schoolteacher, Master Hingston, and known locally as "The Master's House". Tucked into the folds of a hollow and modestly restored, it is not just a fine place to stay, but is also home to a computer software company – Empathy, which Chris runs – and is a house where one of the main attractions – aside from the calmness and the intellectual vigour of your hosts – also offers splendiferous regional French cuisine, cooked by Joelle.

Mrs Johnson is a Breton, spent time living on the banks of the Loire, and her menus range freely through the classic dishes of her native land, "using the very best ingredients to be found on the Dingle peninsula cooked in the tradition of regional France": Fromage de tete. Gigot d'agneau a la languedocienne. Escalope de poulet Vallée d'Auge. Pipérade. Tarte tatin.

"It's like a French special occasion dinner in a home", says Joêlle, who is unduly modest about her skills, a modesty her guests know disguises a fine talent, at work in a fine house.

● **OPEN:**
All year
● **ROOMS:**
Thee double bedrooms, two single rooms
● **AVERAGE PRICE:**
B&B £17 per person. B&B + Dinner £31 per person

● **NOTES:**
Dinner 7.30pm-8.30pm, communal table
Enclosed Car Parking. No Wheelchair Access
Babies and Children over 10 yrs welcome, cot
high chair
From Killarney turn left at Farranfore, right into
Castlemaine, left for Dingle, Inch, then follow sign for
Dingle. At Lispole take the first right after the church
and Maxol garage (ask in Garage).

HAWTHORN HOUSE
Noel & Mary O'Brien
Shelbourne Street
Kenmare
Co Kerry
Tel: (064) 41035 Fax: 41932

Mary O'Brien comes from a family which ran the Central Hotel for 25 years, and this expertise in the people business is richly evident in her work. Hawthorn is a homey house, quite simple, but vitally personable.

"When people arrive, they are coming into my home, and this makes it important for you", says Mary. Her greeting is true and vivid, and sets the tone of Hawthorn. You are here to have a good time, and have a good time is what you will certainly do.

The bedrooms are pastel and pretty, not at all overdone, but instead serene and amenable, and there is even a honeymoon suite. The idea of a honeymoon in this sweet house in this sweet town is rather delectable, so go on, make the proposal.

Hawthorn House feels just the way a good B&B should, its nature set by the energy and capability of the owner, its comfort appropriately comforting for the traveller at the end of a long day touring, the breakfast ambience optimistic and promising, the intimacy of the house quickly making friends of all your fellow guests.

It is fine value also, which completes the picture of a place to fondly return to.

● **OPEN:**
All year, except Xmas
● **ROOMS:**
Eight rooms
All en-suite
● **AVERAGE PRICE:**
B&B £19-£23 per person sharing
£5 single supplement

● **NOTES:**
No Dinner (many restaurants locally)
Enclosed Car Parking
No Wheelchair Access
Children – welcome, high chair, cot
● In the centre of Kenmare, between the two entrances to the Park Hotel.

ISKEROON
Geraldine & David Hare
Iskeroon, Caherdaniel, Co Kerry
Tel: (066) 75119 Fax: 75119
e-mail: iskeroon@iol.ie
website: http://homepages.iol.ie/~iskeroon/

David Hare had always known Iskeroon from his holidays in Kerry as a kid, and despite the fact that the Earl of Dunraven built this house as long ago as 1936, David and Geraldine became the first full-time residents when they bought the house three years ago.

It is a marvellous place, mixing elements of Lutyens with New England style and features of the Arts & Crafts movement into something quite special. With lot of horizontal planking which has been painted in bold, rich colours from Fired Earth, the rooms seem to swallow you up.

Its location is equally delectable, at the bottom of the hill down which you take all the left turns until you eventually drive across a small pebble beach, and there it is. But it is marvellously protected from the elements, and you look out at the wild sea from the comfort of the house and feel even better to be here, snuggled up.

Geraldine's cooking concentrates on fish, and guests tend to explore local restaurants after having dinner on the first night. At a time when so much regrettable building is taking place on the Ring of Kerry, a design jewel like Iskeroon is even more valuable.

● **OPEN:**
1 Mar-30 Nov
● **ROOMS:**
Three rooms, all with private bathrooms
● **AVERAGE PRICE:**
B&B £30 per person sharing, £8 single supplement

● **NOTES:**
Dinner, 8.30pm £18 (book by noon)
Bring Your Own Wine
No Wheelchair Access
Children – by arrangement only
● Between Caherdaniel and Waterville, at the Scarriff Inn, turn to Bunavalla Pier. Go to pier, bear left at each bend. At pier turn left through "private" gate, cross beach and enter through white gate posts.

10 WEBSITES TO VISIT

①
http://www.iol.ie/ballvolan/

②
http://commerce.ie/ballynahinch

③
http://homepages.iol.ie/~iskeroon/

④
http://www.parkkenmare.com

⑤
http://indigo.ie/culintra

⑥
http://www.tinakilly.ie

⑦
http://www.clon.ie/letterco.html

⑧
http://www.lissard.com

⑨
http://www.theclarence.ie

⑩
http://www.slh.com/slh/pages/i/ianirea.html

NOTE You can e-mail Estragon Press with your comments at: estragon@iol.ie

THE OLD STONE HOUSE

Michael & Becky O'Connor
Cliddaun, Dingle, Co Kerry
Tel: (066) 59882
Fax: 69882
e-mail: innkeeper@oconnor.ie

Michael and Becky O'Connor's 1864 farmhouse is the kind of place you want to find when touring the exotic and uncontainable delights of County Kerry.

A cosy, small – there are only three bedrooms – and satisfyingly intimate house, its proximity to Dingle allows one to enjoy the frothy recuperations which that town offers, whilst being set out on the road to Ventry means that one is ideally situated to explore County Kerry.

Kerry is an almost unknowable place. It can be possible to look down the valleys and across the hills and to see three entirely different vistas simultaneously within an eyesight, possible to think you have the measure of the place only to realise that there are as many other aspects left unknown as you have come to understand.

No one knows more about the area than Michael O'Connor, and he is a fascinating student of the place and its people, so staying in The Old Stone House means that one can get a true appreciation of this most intractable and romantic place. You should take your time exploring the peninsula, allowing your breath to be taken by scenery which is nothing less than awe-inspiring.

● **OPEN:**
All year except 24-25 Dec
● **ROOMS:**
Three rooms sharing bathroom
● **AVERAGE PRICE:**
B&B £20-£25 per person sharing
£5 single supplement

● **NOTES:**
No Dinner
Enclosed Car Parking
No Wheelchair Access
Children – welcome, cot, high chair, price reduction if sharing
● From Dingle, follow signs for Slea Head Drive. The house is 4km west of Dingle town, on the right. There is a sign at the roadside.

THE PARK HOTEL ✪
Francis Brennan
Kenmare, Co Kerry
Tel: (064) 41200
Fax: 41402
e-mail: phkenmare@iol.ie
website: http://www.parkkenmare.com

They have a simple ambition in The Park Hotel, a simple animus which drives every effort of Francis Brennan and his team. They want to make your stay here not merely memorable, not merely as perfect as they can manage. They actually want to make it unforgettable.

They want you to leave saying to yourself: this is the crème de la crème. And I am the lucky cat who got the crème.

A noble ambition, for sure but, of course, unless they had the wherewithal to achieve it, it would be meaningless. They have that wherewithal.

When you meet Mr Brennan – and The Park is one of few hotels where you will certainly meet the proprietor – he seems relaxed, charming, in charge.

Charming and in charge he is, but don't be fooled by the relaxed nature, for here is a man who is driven by a ferocious desire to be the best, and for whom second place won't do.

He is the best, however, the King in the Kingdom of Kerry, a beneficent despot in his own empire. And The Park is just the perfect place to showcase the skills of Mr Brennan and his team, skills which take care of every detail, unforgettably.

● **OPEN:**
Apr-end Oct (open for Xmas period)
● **ROOMS:**
Forty-nine rooms, all en-suite
● **AVERAGE PRICE:**
B&B £105-£128 per person sharing

● **NOTES:**
Dinner 7pm-8.45pm, £39, separate tables
Car Parking
No Wheelchair Access
Children – welcome, cots, high chair, baby listening, early dinner in room for toddlers
● At the top of the town.

SALLYPORT HOUSE
Arthur family
Glengarriff Road
Kenmare
Tel: (064) 42066
Fax: 41752

Sallyport looks like a new house, a spankingly smart big place just across from the pier as you drive east out of Kenmare town, but Jennie Arthur's house has a long history, despite its modern appearance, and her mother took guests in as long ago as 1967. The house is named for the Sally Port, a stretch of water which runs directly behind the house.

It is a pristine home, its immaculate exterior matched by a meticulous interior. In character, indeed, it is unlike most Irish homes which take guests, the plushness of the house giving it something of that stilled quietude which one finds in self-consciously expensive private hotels in the major cities.

Though only a stone's throw from Kenmare, its serene calmness seems a million miles from that fine, gadabout place. As such, for those who want to party early in the evening before heading home to get a good night's shut-eye, it maybe the perfect location: it comes as little surprise to hear that most of Sallyport's guests are Americans, who appreciate this modest luxury. There are 5 bedrooms, each furnished differently with antique furniture, one of which enjoys a four-poster bed.

● **OPEN:**
Easter-Nov
● **ROOMS:**
Five rooms, all with bathrooms
● **AVERAGE PRICE:**
B&B £35-£40 per person sharing

● **NOTES:**
No Dinner
Enclosed Car Parking
No Wheelchair Access
Not suitable for Children
● From Killarney follow Glengarriff signpost through Kenmare and Sallyport House is on your left just after the bridge in Kenmare, coming from the direction of Glengarriff.

SHELBURNE LODGE ✪
Tom & Maura Foley
Killowen, Cork Road
Kenmare
Co Kerry
Tel: (064) 41013
Fax: 42135

"Walls are for hanging pictures and for framing furniture", says Maura Foley, and in Shelburne Lodge she has found the perfect canvas for two of her three passions.

Her first passion is for cooking, in which guise she runs Packies, in the town of Kenmare, and produces some of the finest food to be enjoyed in Ireland.

Her second passion is for interior design, at which she exhibits such an intuitive, original perspective that she has created a house which ranks right up there with the other great and gorgeous houses of Ireland. "Sometimes I think it's really what I should have concentrated on", says Maura.

Working on the template of a fine Georgian farmhouse, Mrs Foley has radicalised the interior, using massive mirrors to intensify the sense of space, and otherwise hanging and framing works of art and idiosyncratic furniture to achieve a grace and favour everywhere you look.

For it is her third passion, for appreciating and enjoying beautiful things, which has allowed Maura Foley to create a house with such depth and concentration. Shelburne is a shrine to good taste, to judgement, to intelligence and, like Maura Foley's cooking, it wears all these virtues with ease.

● **OPEN:**
1 Apr-30 Oct
● **ROOMS:**
Seven rooms, all en-suite
● **AVERAGE PRICE:**
B&B £25-£40 per person sharing

● **NOTES:**
No Dinner (good restaurants locally)
Enclosed Car Parking
No Wheelchair Access
Children – welcome, high chair, cot
● 300 yards from Kenmare, across from the golf course on the Cork road.

TONLEGEE HOUSE

Mark & Marjorie Molloy
Athy, Co Kildare
Tel: (0507) 31473 Fax: 31473
e-mail: tonlegeehouse@tinet.ie

Marjorie and Mark Molloy are one of the best twosomes in the people business in Ireland.

Mr Molloy keeps a low profile, for the most part, staying in the kitchen and letting his cooking speak for itself. And here is cooking which can sing a melody of deliciously contrived, expertly controlled flavours. If Mr Molloy cooked up in the capital, he would be justly famous. Down here in Kildare, he just gets on with the job, doing it well, doing it right.

Mrs Molloy, meantime, works the front of house and oversees this elegant house, dating from 1750, with a charm which is charged with an effortless efficiency. She has the command of a French Madame, and a spontaneity which is priceless.

A few years back, an English traveller wrote to us, choosing from amongst a variety of Bridgestone destinations the pleasures of Tonlegee.

"I should like particularly to congratulate the Molloys. Nothing was ever too much trouble, and the food was exceptional", she wrote. Generous compliments, for sure, but no more than this sparky, clever couple deserve. Tonlegee is their space, their stage, and they tread its boards with a confident professionalism which is a joy.

● **OPEN:**
all year except 2 weeks in late autumn
● **ROOMS:**
Nine rooms, all en-suite
● **AVERAGE PRICE:**
B&B £35 per person sharing
£10 single supplement

● **NOTES:**
Dinner 7pm-9pm Mon-Thur, 7pm-10.30pm Fri-Sat, £22
No Wheelchair Access
Children – welcome
● Leave Athy, crossing over Barrow Bridge and Canal Bridge. You will see Tegral on your left, take the next left turn and the house is just around the bend.

BERRYHILL
George & Belinda Dyer
Berryhill, Inistioge
Co Kilkenny
Tel: (056) 58434
Fax: 58434

Berryhill is the sort of house which seems not merely snugly ensconced, but snugly embedded, in the lush countryside of Kilkenny. George and Belinda Dyer's house is one of those places which introduces you to the sort of pleasures you quickly want to make a permanent feature of your life.

For it is not just the droll humour of the decorations in the frog suite, or the pig room, or the elephant collection which captivates. It is the bath by firelight.

If you take the elephant room, the downstairs room of the three which the house offers, then you may well find after you return from an evening out, that the fire in the bathroom is blazing away. What could be nicer, as you sink into the suds, than to have the flicker of flame warming and dancing about the room as you soak off the pleasures of the day, abandoned altogether to the seductive simplicity of the whole thing.

You find that people who stay here are quickly at their ease, having another slug of something potent from the drinks trolley, gaustering away long into the morning at breakfast time, as the bumper breakfasts unfold.

● **OPEN:**
1 Apr-mid Nov
● **ROOMS:**
Three rooms, all en-suite
● **AVERAGE PRICE:**
B&B £40 per person sharing
£10 single supplement

● **NOTES:**
Dinner, £25, for parties of 4-6 by request only, communal table
No Wheelchair Access
Children – over ten welcome
Enclosed car parking
● From Inistioge, cross the bridge, bearing right, take the next left, then the next right and the house is the second on the left.

CULLINTRA HOUSE
Patricia Cantlon
The Rower, Inistioge, Co Kilkenny
Tel: (051) 423614
e-mail: cullhse@indigo/ie
website: http://indigo.ie/cullintra

In many ways, Patricia Cantlon's lovely farmhouse operates rather like an old fashioned salon. The centre of the operation at Cullintra is the lady herself – hostess, and entertainment, and conductor of the assembled guests. Things are done Ms Cantlon's way, and at Ms Cantlon's speed.

Some folk don't really like this, as you might expect. In a world where many travellers expect pretty much the same sort of thing from every place they visit – the television in the room, the room service, the prompt timekeeping of an hotel dining room, the damned trouser press – these travellers can turn up at this lovely farmhouse and wonder just what on earth has happened to them.

What has happened to them is simple. They have stepped out of the normal, workaday world, into Patricia Cantlon's world, her salon, which operates at a different pace, operates according to different strokes. Here, the host is no mere factotum, but an integral part of the experience, eccentricities and all. If the homogenised travellers don't like what they find, it is their loss. You are out of time, out of the real world, in this little salon with your fellow travellers. It's bizarre, but it is quite real.

● **OPEN:**
All year
● **ROOMS:**
Six rooms, three en-suite
● **AVERAGE PRICE:**
B&B £25 per person sharing. £10 single supplement

● **NOTES:**
No Credit Cards accepted
Dinner after 9pm, £16, three communal tables
Enclosed car parking
No Wheelchair Access
Children – welcome, cots but no high chairs and no babysitting service
● Six miles from New Ross on the Kilkenny Road.

LACKEN HOUSE
Eugene & Breda McSweeney
Dublin Road, Kilkenny, Co Kilkenny
Tel: (056) 61085, Fax: 62435
e-mail: lackenhs@indigo.ie

The word "Welcome" is carved in stained glass over the front door at Lacken House, a small country hotel on the edge of Kilkenny town, and the McSweeneys – husband and wife, chef and sommelier, Eugene and Breda, take the business of welcome seriously, and their entire métier is dedicated to creating a place where their skills are put at the service of your needs.

Bedrooms are small with tiny en suite bathrooms, but they don't miss a thing when it comes to comfort, including televisions, tea trays and the sort of glossy magazines on wine and fashion you only get to read in the dentist – only these ones are up-to-date.

Downstairs in the small, romantic dining room Eugene corrals the efforts of local farmers, cheesemakers, and other artisans into tremendous dinners which bear the stamp of one of the best, and most original, cooks in the country.

To feel genuinely welcome in an hotel it takes much more than simple warmth and courtesy. It takes thought to anticipate your needs, and skill to cater for them. Lacken House works hard to ensure that the word "Welcome" over the door is not just a word in a window, it's a true feeling.

● **OPEN:**
All year except 1 week at Xmas
● **ROOMS:**
Eight rooms, all en-suite
● **AVERAGE PRICE:**
B&B £30 per person sharing
£36 single

● **NOTES:**
Dinner 7pm-10.30pm, Tue-Sat
Enclosed Car Parking
No Wheelchair Access
Children – welcome, high chair, cot
● On the Dublin road, just as you drive into Kilkenny from Carlow, just past the roundabout on the right hand side of the road.

CHEZ NOUS
Audrey & Tony Canavan
Kilminchy
Portlaoise
Co Laois
Tel: (0502) 21251

Every single thing in every single place in Audrey
Canavan's lovely bungalow is garlanded and glorified, gar-
nished and arranged, fretted and patterned. Enhanced,
enriched, embellished, here is Irish vernacular design aug-
mented with the voluptuousness of Gothic and adminis-
tered with roccoco unrestraint. It's wonderful.

It is a classic of Irish domestic vernacular design, and to
this classic Audrey Canavan brings a welcome so spontaneous and genuine that it soothes the heart, and disarms
your cares.

For a night, you are back in the realm of innocence, the
little doll in the little doll's house. In truth, Chez Nous is
a little like a doll's house, so pristine and perfect, so
orchestrated and controlled. Is this why one sleeps so
well when staying here? You seem less like an adult, with
adult cares, and are suddenly more like a child, whose
vision descends to immaculate simplicity.

At breakfast, the breakfast plate with its bounteous offer-
ings will be plashed with edible flowers, all the better to
help you to enjoy your bumper potato cakes with lash-
ings of butter and sea salt, or Clonakilty pudding cooked
in duck fat, or deep-fried mozzarella, or kippers with
scrambled eggs, or trout with almonds and parsley.

● **OPEN:**
Jan 3-Dec 20
● **ROOMS:**
Five rooms, four en-suite
● **AVERAGE PRICE:**
B&B £18-£25 per person sharing
£5 single supplement

● **NOTES:**
No Credit Cards accepted.
High tea, 6.30pm, £12.50, if pre booked
No Wheelchair Access
Children – over 8yrs welcome
● Chez Nous is 2.5km from the town centre, signpost-
ed from the Dublin/Portlaoise road.

PRESTON HOUSE
Allison Dowling
Main Street, Abbeyleix
Co Laois
Tel: (0502) 31432
Fax: 31432

We all have an idyllic vision of that perfect on-the-major-road place, a restaurant with rooms, someplace where we will find good food, a good welcome, a good bottle of wine, a good bed for the night.

It is the sort of place we think of when it is late, dark, probably raining. And then you find yourself in the lovely village of Abbeyleix. And at the southern end of the village is a sign which says "Preston House". You pull over, note the ageless façade of a building which used to be a boys' school, walk through the door, spy the simple gingham tablecloths, note the interesting aromas snaking from the kitchen and the casual ambience of the place, and think: "This is it".

And, yes it is. Allison and Michael Dowling's restaurant with rooms, right on the busiest road in the entire country, is a traveller's beacon. Upstairs there are comfy, sleepy bedrooms. Downstairs there is a small restaurant, with Mrs Dowling's lovely, tasty cooking to be enjoyed: some smoked haddock chowder; roast honey duckling with a red plum and port sauce, or maybe some fine sirloin with mushrooms and tomatoes; and then a hot chocolate soufflé. Splendid, perfect.

● **OPEN:**
All year (except Xmas)
● **ROOMS:**
Four rooms, all en-suite
● **AVERAGE PRICE:**
B&B £25 per person sharing
£5 single supplement

● **NOTES:**
Open Tue-Sat 10am-9pm,
Sun lunch only if pre-booked.
Limited hours off season.
Reservations always helpful, advise Allison on your requirements when booking.
No Wheelchair Access
Children – welcome, high chair, cot
● On the main street in Abbeyleix (the main Dublin/Cork road).

ROUNDWOOD HOUSE
Frank & Rosemary Kennan
Mountrath, Co Laois
Tel: (0502) 32120 Fax: 32711
roundwood@tinet.ie

Towards the end of a fine dinner one night in Roundwood House, an Englishman asked those sitting at the communal dinner table, "Why do we come to Ireland?". His fellow guests, who up to then had been somewhat taciturn due to unfamiliarity with English, were suddenly transformed.

"The soft rain, the green grass, the cow in the field" said the lady from Hanover. "The friendly people, the welcome, the taste of the food", said the couple from Bavaria. "The humanity, the respect, the calm", said the folk from London.

It was all a little like a dream, composed as the sentiments were of such hallowed clichés about Ireland and the Irish. But there was not a jot of irony about any of the remarks. Remarkable as this may have been, the visitors were actually overlooking why they were having such a high old time. They were having such a high old time because they were in Roundwood, eating Rosemary Kennan's lovely cooking, and because Roundwood is a house which can cast a spell on you.

Here is a Palladian house which does not tend or pretend to the pristine. It is old and rather lovely, and it is lovely to stay here.

● **OPEN:**
All year except Xmas Day
● **ROOMS:**
Ten rooms, all en-suite
● **AVERAGE PRICE:**
B&B £38 per person sharing
£8 single supplement

● **NOTES:**
Dinner 8.30pm, £22, communal table
(separate table available if guests vehemently protest)
No Wheelchair Access
Children – welcome, high chair, cot, babysitting
● At entry to Mountrath turn right at T-junction for Ballyfin and left again immediately onto R440 for Slieve Bloom Mountains. 3 miles exactly on R440.

HOLLYWELL
Rosaleen & Tom Maher
Liberty Hill, Carrick-on-Shannon
Co Leitrim
Tel: (078) 21124
Fax: 21124

Hospitality is in the blood of Tom and Rosaleen Maher. Mr Maher hails from a hotel-keeping family, and for part of the year he trains youngsters in the art of people handling via the state agency, CERT.

Perhaps it is this mixture of the practical and the academic which explains Hollywell's confident, capacious grace. It is a truly welcoming house, the sort of place which feels like home from the minute you walk through the front door.

The furnishings suit the grand-but-modest size of the house, whilst the breakfast room is wisely focused on the view of the River Shannon. On a summer morning, it feels like a mighty privilege to take breakfast here, with light glinting off the slow-running river and, with lovely fresh fruits and good baked ham and fine cheeses and warm bread and good coffee, it transpires to become a feast, just right to set you up for a day on the Shannon-Erne waterway, doing a whole lot of nothing very much whatsoever. Hollywell is also a perfect base for exploring this unspoilt area.

Tom and Rosaleen see to everything in Hollywell with a practiced eye, and their assurance practically guarantees a good time in this fine house.

● **OPEN:**
All year, except Xmas
● **ROOMS:**
Four rooms, all en-suite
● **AVERAGE PRICE:**
B&B £27-£35 per person sharing
£8-£10 single supplement

● **NOTES:**
No Dinner
Enclosed Car Park
No Wheelchair Access
Children over 12yrs welcome
● From Carrick-on-Shannon, cross the bridge, keep left at Gings Pub. The entrance to Holl;ywell in on the left.

BALLYTEIGUE HOUSE
Margaret & Dick Johnson
Bruree, nr Charleville, Co Limerick
Tel: (063) 90575 Fax: 90575

You have just vaulted the Atlantic in a jet, picked up a hire car and motored the sixty minutes from Shannon airport to Ballyteigue House. You are sitting in the drawing room in front of a hungry, bright fire, and you cannot believe your luck.

If this is Ireland, you already want more of it. At the very least, you want more of Ballyteigue House and are probably planning to pass your last night here, in the bosom of the Lee valley, looking out at the placid vista which sweeps away from the house.

A high, wide, handsome house which is comfortable and inexpensive, this is a place in which to do nothing very much whatsoever – flop in front of the fire with a mind-emptying mag, nap away the afternoon, focus on dinner for an hour beforehand – or you could shoot and fish and do other estimable sporty fixations should that be to your taste. Margaret Johnson makes it rather difficult to drag yourself away from the house however. She is a ter-rifically sociable woman, who makes you feel welcome in about thirty seconds flat, whether you are jet-jaundiced and road-weary, or bright-eyed and holiday-moded. Whatever your motivations Ballyteigue is somewhere splendid.

● **OPEN:**
All year, except Xmas. Booking essential off season.
● **ROOMS:**
Five rooms, four en-suite, 1 single room with private bathroom
● **AVERAGE PRICE:**
B&B £18-£23 per person sharing
£18 single

● **NOTES:**
Dinner 7pm, £16, set menu
No Wheelchair Access
Children – welcome, cot, high chair, babysitting, 50% dis-count when sharing room.
● 2km off the N20. Take first right after O'Rourke's Cross going south. Pass Rockhill on right and watch for sign.

THE MUSTARD SEED
AT ECHO LODGE ✪
Daniel F. Mullane
Ballingarry, Co Limerick
Tel: (069) 68508
Fax: 68511

In contrast to those who believe that the object of spending a million quid on a house is to ensure that everyone sees where every penny has been spent, Dan Mullane's Echo Lodge is almost demure.

Here, the intrinsic aesthetic of each thing – the ticking which decorates some of the chairs, the garden architecture prints in the library, the contemplative warmth of the hallway dedicated to diverse religions – is revealed, and then congratulated, by the other objects around it. "The house feels like it has been here for ever", says Mr Mullane.

The use of colour, for example, works here because at times its use is restrained, and then suddenly the bright shock from the Villeroy and Bosch plates will leap out at you. There are few paintings throughout the house, but the use of photographs, prints, and covers from magazines such as American "Gourmet", works perfectly – slightly ironic, and yet effective.

Though it is a public house, the house still feels like a private space, thanks to the use of prized – rather than merely valuable – objects, and so we feel we are in the presence of little pieces, little fragments, of Mr Mullane's personal history. A wonderful house.

● **OPEN:**
Mar-Jan, except Xmas
● **ROOMS:**
Twelve rooms, all en-suite
● **AVERAGE PRICE:**
B&B £50-£75per person sharing
£15 single supplement

● **NOTES:**
Dinner 7pm-9.45pm, £30, separate tables
Full Wheelchair Access
Children – welcome, high chair, cot
● Take the Killarney road from Adare. Quarter mile from Adare take the first turning to left (R519). Follow signs to Ballingarry and house is signposted.

REENS FARMHOUSE
Tilly Curtin
Ardagh
Co Limerick
Tel: (069) 64276

Seen from the road, Reens Farmhouse looks rather dramatic and imposing, with a long straight driveway lined by trees culminating in a fine, stone house, with a grand conservatory wrapping itself around the entrance.

But, once inside, any element of hauteur is dispensed, as Tilly Curtin takes you into her care and brews some tea and, next morning, makes a cracking fry-up. Mrs Curtin belongs to that school of devoted and talented B&B keepers who are as dotey and delightful as a storybook granny. Surrender yourself into her care and your cares vanish amidst the pristine housekeeping and voluble friendliness of Reens farmhouse.

Reens is, like the other cuddly-granny B&B's you will find in this book, almost a definition of spontaneous, genuine, charming Irish hospitality. The style of the house is a pure spit 'n' polish Irish vernacular, quickly comfortable, and it is all too easy to linger over breakfast around the great big table, as you chat with the other guests, and discuss the state of the world. Or at least that tiny little bit of it which is a few miles north of Abbeyfeale and a few miles south of Newcastle West, and which you all want to come back to.

● **OPEN:**
15 Apr-30 Sept
● **ROOMS:**
Four rooms,
Two en-suite
● **AVERAGE PRICE:**
B&B £20 per person sharing
£5 single supplement

● **NOTES:**
No Dinner
No Wheelchair Access
Children – welcome, high chair, cot, baby monitor
● Situated on the N21, the main Limerick to Killarney and Tralee road, 31/2 miles from underpass in Rathkeale and 4 miles from Newcastle West. Do not go into Ardagh.

JORDAN'S TOWNHOUSE AND RESTAURANT

Harry & Marian Jordan
Newry Street, Carlingford, Co Louth
Tel: (042) 73223
Fax: 73827

Carlingford is a village which is on a roll, and Jordan's is one of the reasons why.

Along with other places in this quixotic village, it has a spontaneous wit and charm you won't find outside County Louth, best exemplified by the style of welcome. Because of all the greetings in all the places in all the country, the one we would like to hear most is the one with which Harry Jordan greeted a customer. Shaking the man by the hand, Mr Jordan said simply: "You're as welcome as a fresh egg". Oh, to feel as welcome as a fresh egg!

But that will be just how you feel when resting in Jordan's Townhouse, a fine brace of rooms created out of an old potato shed, just at the rear of their restaurant. The rooms are spacious, with room to stretch out, and the views across Carlingford Lough and across the Mountains of Mourne are splendid.

It is just the sort of little hideaway which, in combination with the romantic, relaxing character of Jordan's restaurant and this engaging village, make for a smashing escape. Its charm inspires pride, the sort of pride which explains why Carlingford is on a roll.

● **OPEN:**
all year (except a few weeks in Jan)
● **ROOMS:**
Five rooms, all en-suite
● **AVERAGE PRICE:**
B&B from £37.50 per person sharing
£7.50 single supplement

● **NOTES:**
Dinner 6.30pm-9.45pm, £22.50
Separate tables
Wheelchair Access
Children – welcome, high chairs, cots, telephone listening service
Locked parking on request
● Centre of Carlingford village

ENNISCOE HOUSE
Susan Kellett
Castlehill, near Crossmolina, Ballina, Co Mayo
Tel: (096) 31112
Fax: 31773
enniscoe@indigo.ie

Where some of the Irish country houses are showy and blowy and priced to match, Susan Kellett's house is demure and unassuming. It may seem oxymoronic to suggest that any substantial country house could be described as "modest". Yet, that is the memory that most comes to mind when one thinks of Enniscoe.

A softly pinky Georgian house which Ms Kellett has carefully and cleverly set to rights, its principal virtue is a gentleness, an other-worldliness, that is disarmingly easy to like. If forced to put your finger on it, you might describe the house as "feminine", both in style and in ambience.

Those bedrooms at the front of the house, overlooking the grounds, are truly the ones you want to reserve when staying, and their quirky four posters and big lazy canopy beds are great fun.

At dinnertime, the use of local foods – including some from the garden – mean that local flavours find their way into play throughout the simple menus. It is country house cooking, of course, but just right, friendly food within a friendly house, and Enniscoe is a place easy to relax in, to enjoy time alone and apart from the real world.

● **OPEN:**
1 Apr-14 Oct
● **ROOMS:**
Six rooms, all en-suite
● **AVERAGE PRICE:**
B&B £44-£50 per person sharing
£5-£10 single supplement

● **NOTES:**
Dinner 8pm-8.30pm, £22
No Wheelchair Access
Children – welcome, high chair, cot, babysitting available
● From Ballina take the road to Crossmolina. In Crossmolina, turn left in the centre of town. Enniscoe gates are 2 miles on left.

NEWPORT HOUSE
Kieran & Thelma Thompson
Newport
Co Mayo
Tel: (098) 41222
Fax: 41613

"People say they feel they have been invited for a country weekend", says Kieran Thompson, and that is just how you will feel, after a spell at Newport.

There is something so confidently, enjoyably patrician in Kieran and Thelma Thompson's formidable house that few others of the Irish country houses can match the elegant understatement of its luxury.

What fascinates the visitor, as much as the baleful calm of the house, is the thrilling kaleidoscope of clichés which it offers for our delectation. The ruddy-cheeked ghillies, who wait around the hallway in the morning, anxious for fishing to begin. The impossibly stooped gardener. The engaging staff with their wise suggestions as to what you might enjoy for dinner. The ageing ladies who wait on the fringes of the dining room and who, should you stay long enough, will elide you under their wings and into their care.

Kieran Thompson describes the culinary philosophy of Newport as "allowing the quality of the food to come out", and John Gavan's food does just that. It is sumptuous food, for the most part, especially their wonderful smoked salmon, but it enjoys the ruddy flavour of their own marvellous vegetables and fine local meats.

● **OPEN:**
19 Mar-end Sept
● **ROOMS:**
Eighteen rooms,
seventeen en-suite
● **AVERAGE PRICE:**
B&B £56-£69 per person sharing low season
£59-£73 high season

● **NOTES:**
Dinner 7pm-9.30pm, £30
Limited Wheelchair Access
Children – welcome, high chair, cot, babysitting
● In the village of Newport.

THE OLD WORKHOUSE
Niamh Colgan
Ballinlough, Dunshaughlin, Co Meath
Tel: (01) 825 9251
Fax: 825 9251

The Old Workhouse was first occupied in 1841, a noble collection of buildings with a three storey tower to the left hand side of the main run of the house, set hard by the road, a mile south of the buzzing and expanding village of Dunshaughlin.

Inside, the Colgans have completely reversed the nature of the place. Where it was once forbidding and foreboding, it is now graceful and super-comfortable. Where once it was a monument to human frailty and indifference, it is now a monument to hospitality and care. The size of the gallery drawingroom and the entrance hall is majestic, the four bedrooms are pastel gentle.

There is a relish in Niamh Colgan's voice when she talks about the food she prepares for guests. The gigot pork chops cooked with orange, one of her specialities. The ham simmered slowly in cider which is set out each morning for breakfast. The fresh fruit and vegetable juices she whizzes up at morningtime. The excellent fruit cake – moist, crumbly – which meets you with a cup of tea when you arrive. She relishes this work, and it shows, and it is the simple thoughtfulness of Mrs Colgan which makes the Workhouse work.

● **OPEN:**
Mid Mar-Nov
● **ROOMS:**
Four rooms, 1 suite
All en-suite
● **AVERAGE PRICE:**
B&B £26-£30 per person sharing
£10 single supplement

● **NOTES:**
Dinner 7.30pm, £22.50
Communal table,
Book dinner by noon
Wheelchair Access to ground floor rooms
Children – welcome, but no reduction in price
● On the main N3, Dublin Cavan road, one mile on the Dublin side of Dunshaughlin.

HILTON PARK ✪
Johnny & Lucy Madden
Clones, Co Monaghan
Tel: (047) 56007 Fax: 56033
e-mail: hilton@tempoweb.com
website: http://www.temporweb.com/hilton/

There is nowhere else like Hilton Park. Nowhere else where the scale of a house is so grand, nowhere else where the sense of entering the architecture and style of the past is so profound, nowhere else where the intellectual incisiveness of the owners plays such a large part in the pleasures of the house, and there is nowhere else where the cooking is so appropriate. It is a place unto itself, strange and strangely wonderful.

Johnny and Lucy Madden assemble all the elements of this monumental place with great skill and wisdom. Mrs Madden's splendid book of potato recipes, "The Potato Year", is a brilliant collection of recipes, with a dish for every day of the year, and as such it is a pointer to her determined nature. Mr Madden complements his wife's intensity with a patrician calm.

Above all, in Hilton the cooking is thrilling: a warm salad of monkfish with butter-fried purple sage, buckler's sorrel, raddiccio and hazelnut oil; medallions of lamb cooked with basil and tomato with tiny fir apple potatoes and char-grilled courgettes; a fine cheeseboard, then hot apricot shortbread with poached peaches. Hilton Park is a classic of the genre.

● **OPEN:**
1 Apr-30 Sep
● **ROOMS:**
Six rooms, all en-suite
● **AVERAGE PRICE:**
B&B £52-£67.50 per person sharing
£10 single supplement

● **NOTES:**
Dinner 8pm precisely, £25
24 hours notice required if having dinner
No Wheelchair Access
Children – over 8 yrs welcome. Enclosed car parking
● From Clones take the Scotshouse road and the gates (dark green with silver falcons) are on the right after 3 miles.

10 GREAT HOUSES FOR WEEKENDS

①

ASSOLAS HOUSE
KANTURK, CO CORK

②

HANORA'S COTTAGE
CLONMEL, CO WATERFORD

③

HILTON PARK
CLONES, CO MONAGHAN

④

JORDANS TOWNHOUSE
CARLINGFORD, CO LOUTH

⑤

KELLY'S RESORT HOTEL
ROSSLARE, CO WEXFORD

⑥

LONGUEVILLE
MALLOW, CO CORK

⑦

SALVILLE HOUSE
ENNISCORTHY, CO WEXFORD

⑧

TEMPLE
MOATE, CO WESTMEATH

⑨

ROUNDWOOD HOUSE
MOUNTRATH, CO LAOIS

⑩

TINAKILLY HOUSE
RATHNEW, CO WICKLOW

SPINNERS TOWNHOUSE & BISTRO

Joe & Fiona Breen, Siobhan Hoare
Castle Street, Birr, Co Offaly
Tel: (0509) 21673 Fax: 21673

"At Spinners we celebrate the landscape and visual inspiration of the Irish Midlands", say Joe and Fiona Breen, and it is no idle boast.

This is a clever establishment, an astute and democratic mix of rooms culled from what were originally 5 Georgian houses. In developing them, the Breens have created a lively, characterful space which shows restraint – in the careful selection of furniture and the simplicity of the rooms – and zest – canvases by various Irish painters jump out from the walls, whilst access to the enclosed courtyard breathes both a great deal of light and spaciousness into the townhouse.

The most recent elaboration to the house has been the opening of Spinners Bistro, where Siobhan Hoare cooks an eclectic, funky style of food which reveals the background of someone who worked in The Ramore Restaurant, in Portrush, and out in Australia.

Grilled tiger prawns. Confit of duck with Drambuie. Tagliatelle with smoked salmon. Salmon and potato cakes with a dill seed mayonnaise. It's impressive cooking, served in a charming room, and it is excellent value for money. The Bistro, like the Townhouse, has lots of personality, and this is Spinners great gift. It is imaginative, and refreshingly unclichéd.

● **OPEN:**
Mid Mar-Dec
● **ROOMS:**
Eight rooms & one dorm
Five en-suite
● **AVERAGE PRICE:**
B&B dorm £10
£17.50 per person sharing
£2.50 single supplement

● **NOTES:**
Dinner 6pm-10pm
Wheelchair Access
Children – welcome, cots, high chair, babysitting
● Beside the castle in Birr.

COOPERSHILL HOUSE

Brian & Lindy O'Hara
Riverstown, Co Sligo
Tel: (071) 65108
e-mail: ohara@coopershill.com

Few other of the country houses in Ireland can provoke the unguarded affection which settles into the hearts of the guests you will meet at Coopershill. The travellers, holidaymakers and weekenders who love Brian and Lindy O'Hara's Georgian mansion love it madly, with many of them returning to Sligo on an annual pilgrimage of pleasure. For private house parties, it is one of the optimum choices out of season.

The house has been home to seven generations of the O'Haras since it was built in 1774, and one can only surmise, given its meticulous, understated, pristine condition, that the O'Haras are magnificent housekeepers, for Coopershill looks as if it was built yesterday. All a-gleam and a-glisten, it is a tribute to hard work, and to a vision of a country house as a living space, not a mere repository of archaic values and archaic furniture.

Brian's bashful sense of humour and Lindy's good cooking complete the picture of a special house. She does classic dishes such as wild salmon with a hollandaise to perfection, and there are lovely things like smoked sea trout with quail's eggs and a lemon butter sauce, casserole of venison in red wine, bumper desserts such as baked stuffed nectarines with mango ice cream, or a rich pecan pie. Just the right food in just the right house.

● **OPEN:**
Mar-1 Nov
● **ROOMS:**
Eight rooms, all with private bathrooms
● **AVERAGE PRICE:**
B&B £45-£52 per person sharing
£10 single supplement

● **NOTES:**
Dinner 8.30pm, £18-£25
6.30pm-8pm Sun, £25-£35
No Wheelchair Access
Children – welcome
● Coopershill is clearly signposted from the Drumfin crossroads on the N4, 11 miles southwest of Sligo.

CROMLEACH LODGE
Christy and Moira Tighe
Ballindoon, Boyle, Co Sligo
Tel: (071) 65155 Fax: 65455
e-mail: cromleac@iol.ie

Neither Christy nor Moira Tighe have a background in the business of running a restaurant with rooms, and it is their individual, unclichéd way of working which has made Cromleach celebrated.

From a distance the house itself is a curiosity, the sum of steady accretions over the years, with the original building now difficult to detect amidst the extra rooms which have been added. Curiously, the overall effect is not unlike a building intent on creating an organic relationship with its site.

The bedrooms upstairs are super-large and super-comfortable, with heartbreak views across fields that appear to have been purloined from a painting by Breughel, and on and out across Lough Arrow and the gorgeous Curlew Mountains. From the comfort of the modern, you gaze upon the rustic.

Moira Tighe's cooking exploits two central themes: impeccable ingredients from local growers, and cooking which, despite the fact that she is self taught, strides confidently between modern improvisations and the classic verities where her work can seem most confidently at home. Whatever she does, this is a cook with personality and Cromleach is a house powered by Christy and Moira, and their determination to do things right.

● **OPEN:**
Feb-Nov
● **ROOMS:**
Ten rooms, all en-suite
● **AVERAGE PRICE:**
B&B £59-£89 per person sharing
£30 single supplement

● **NOTES:**
Dinner 7pm-9pm Mon-Sat
6.30pm-8pm Sun, £25-£35
No Wheelchair Access
Children – welcome, high chair, cot, babysitting, private family dining room
● Signposted from Castlebaldwin on the N4.

GLEBE HOUSE
Brid and Marc Torrades
Coolaney Road, Collooney, Co Sligo
Tel: (071) 67787 Fax: 80433
e-mail: glebehse@iol.ie

Brid and Marc Torrades read a newspaper article about Glebe House, then a splendid ruin in Collooney, near Sligo, and with the wild energy of youth they migrated to the west coast to bring the unruly ruin back to some kind of shape.

By August 1990, they were open for business, quickly achieving popularity amongst the well-fed citizens of Sligo and further afield. That quiet fame is well founded, for Ms Torrades allies a tenderly feminine skill as a cook with a rock-solid appreciation of fresh ingredients, most of them grown in the garden by Marc.

She cooks with great motivation, with the rustic element of cuisine bourgeois perhaps most at home in her culinary scheme: leg of lamb with Madeira, or sautéed beef with wild mushrooms and garlic are lovable confections of hers, the kind of dishes you want to eat on autumn evenings, and her vegetable cookery, with magnificent ingredients, is amongst the best you can find. Carrots and parsnips eaten here can be amazing.

The rooms in the house are simple, and inexpensive, and improvements take place steadily. No matter. It is the food and the hospitality and the energetic cheerfulness which is the charm of Glebe.

● **OPEN:**
All year, except Xmas
● **ROOMS:**
Five rooms, all en-suite
● **AVERAGE PRICE:**
B&B £20-£25 per person sharing
£2.50 single supplement
● **CREDIT CARDS:**
Visa, Access/Master, Amex, Diners

● **NOTES:**
Dinner 6.30pm-9.30pm, £18.95
Wheelchair Access
Children – welcome, high chair, cot
● Seven miles from Sligo on the Collooney/Coolaney road.

TEMPLE HOUSE ✪
Sandy and Deb Perceval
Temple House, Ballymote, Co Sligo
Tel: (071) 83329 Fax: 83808
e-mail: temple@tempoweb.com
http://www.tempoweb.com/temple/

The word you most often hear in connection with Temple House is 'perfection'. The ability of Sandy and Deb Perceval, and this hulkingly handsome house, to render people speechless with delight is unchallenged in Ireland. What do people love? The food, says the acclaimed chef. The dinner party atmosphere, say your parents. The whacky and exotic rooms, say your friends, and they list the contents of the Twins' Room: two washbasins, two wash stands, two bed-end tables, two bedside lamps, two bedside polar bear ornaments, two towels, two flannels, two windows and two fine canopied beds. The friendship, say the people who have already been three times. The sport, say the fishermen and the huntsmen. Temple House is all things to all men and women, and all these things spell happiness.

The house itself is undeniably absurd and splendid, but it is the Perceval's gift to remove any strain of preciousness or pretention from Temple House which makes it work. 'They are able to create a real kind of relaxed caring', says the lady from Germany. Yes, that's it.

Do note that one is politely requested to refrain from wearing perfumes, hair sprays, after shaves etc, as they engender a severe allergic reaction in Mr Perceval.

● **OPEN:**
Easter-30 Nov
● **ROOMS:**
Five rooms, all en-suite
● **AVERAGE PRICE:**
B&B £38-£40 per person sharing
£5 single supplement

● **NOTES:**
Dinner 7.30pm, £18, communal table, book by 1pm
No Wheelchair Access
Children – welcome, high chair, cot, high tea, 6.30pm for under fives
● Temple House is 14 miles from Sligo and is signposted from the N17 Sligo to Galway road.

BALLYCORMAC HOUSE
Herb & Christine Quigley
Aglish, Borrisokane, Co Tipperary
Tel: (067) 21129
Fax: 21200

The true passion of Herb and Chris Quigley's Ballycormac House is cooking, and there are few more passionate cooks in Ireland than the Quigleys.

Their combined skills are dazzling. Herb is the baker, and a man of such expertise that he has professional chefs attending his weekend bread baking courses. If you had to survive in Ballycormac on a diet of bread and wine, no problem. Just try that Italian recipe for bread stuffed with peppers: Mmmn!

But you don't have to survive on bread and wine. Chris is the cook, and her food speaks long and loud of someone who is inspired by the kitchen.

Sorrel and red onion art. Roasted rabbit with fennel, onion and pancetta. Beetroot and blackcurrant salad on wilted beet greens. Rack of lamb with three peppercorn crust, served with new potatoes and garlic baked in parchment. Wild blackberry gratin with blackberry ice cream.

No other country house in Ireland offers cooking of such originality and such expertise, food which is intellectually reverberant as well as being just doggone delicious. Ballycormac offers great cooking, enlivened by a profound love of food, and the house itself is a low-slung farmhouse, story-book cute, the rooms pleasingly simple.

● **OPEN:**
All year
● **ROOMS:**
Five rooms, all en-suite
● **AVERAGE PRICE:**
B&B £35 per person sharing
£10 single supplement

● **NOTES:**
Dinner 8pm, £20 Sun-Thur, £24 Fri & Sat, communal table
No Wheelchair Access
Children – welcome, cot
● Take Portumna road out of Borrisokane, for half mile, then take first right and follow signs.

INCH HOUSE
John & Nora Egan
Thurles, Co Tipperary
Tel: (0504) 51261/51348
Fax: 51754

Inch House is a monolithic slab of a building. Tall, square, slate-grey in colour, it has an institutional ambience when first seen.

But, then, you walk up the few steps and in through the front door, and suddenly you are embraced by the warm red and blue light streaming through the arching stained glass, and by the sight of a snaking stairway.

You turn right, and walk into a drawing room straight out of that mystical child's imagination which spells William Morris. Across the hallway, the breakfast room is washed with the soft morning light of Tipperary, the perfect location for enjoying breakfast, the perfect place for a convivial dinner.

That you will enjoy breakfast is undoubted, not just for the fine compotes, and the freshly baked breads, and the good eggs, but also for the quiet care of Nora Egan.

Kieran O'Dwyer has charge of the kitchen, and his food enjoys modern flourishes – a warm salad of oatmeal encrusted goat's cheese with yogurt; baked salmon topped with blue poppy seeds served with a beurre blanc – whilst also playing to the strengths of the fine local produce – tenderloin of lamb with a Provençal sauce; sirloin steak with red wine and shallot sauce.

● **OPEN:**
All year, except Xmas
● **ROOMS:**
Five rooms, all en-suite
● **AVERAGE PRICE:**
B&B £25 per person sharing
£5 single supplement

● **NOTES:**
Dinner 7pm-9.30pm Tue-Sat, £23.50, separate tables
No Wheelchair Access
Children – welcome, cot, high chair, babysitting on request
● From Thurles take the top right hand side of the square, Nenagh Road. Drive for 4.5 miles and Inch House is signposted on the left.

TIR NA FUISE
Inez & Niall Heenan
Terryglass, Borrisokane, Co Tipperary
Tel: (067) 22041 Fax: (067) 22041
e-mail: nheenan@tinet.ie

They are real cool guys, Inez and Niall Heenan, brimful of zappy energy and enthusiasm. And it is this very hunger for living, this curiosity in the whys and wherefores of their guests, that makes it such a pleasure to stay in their farmhouse, a few miles from the centre of Terryglass.

Mr Heenan is the farmer, assiduously working a mixed, organic farm which is one of the major attractions of the house, for kids of all ages.

Mrs Heenan is principal of the Gaelscoil, and similarly blessed with an inquisitive, pacific temperament, one of those remarkable women who can do ten things at the same time, and make it seem simple.

The house is simple and delectably comfortable, and there is now a new pair of self-catering cottages renovated from n old stone barn, a wonderful base for exploring this gorgeous part of Tipperary.

Breakfasts are a bumper feast, with every manner of bread and every concoction of egg and fruits available. Best of all, the enthusiasm and spontaneity of Inez and Niall is irresistible, and has already seen them deservedly winning awards for their devoted, dedicated work. A great place.

● **OPEN:**
Easter-Oct 31
● **ROOMS:**
Four rooms, all en-suite
● **AVERAGE PRICE:**
B&B £20 per person sharing
£5 single supplement

● **NOTES:**
No Dinner
No Wheelchair Access
Children – welcome, cot, high chair
● At the crossroads in Borrisokane go straight across, keeping the Centra foodstore on your right, following sign for Ballinderry. In Ballinderry turn right for Terryglass. In Terryglass, turn right and you will see the signpost for the house.

ANNESTOWN HOUSE
John & Pippa Galloway
Annestown, Co Waterford
Tel: (051) 396160 Fax: 396474

You could point to many factors which might explain the attraction of John and Pippa Galloway's house.

It has a smashing location, hard by the sea and adjacent to a sandy beach on this neglected part of the Waterford coastline.

Then, you could identify the attraction as the solid professional background which the Galloways enjoy. It gives their work a confident understatement.

And, of course, Annestown itself is a grand old pile of a Victorian house, its grandeur tempered by the fact that its furnishing is underdone rather than overdone.

But it is definitely the air of nostalgia which clings to the house that makes it special. The sitting room with its flame-lapping fire is the sort of place that demands you sit right down and take tea and cake. The snooker room, ringed with shelf after shelf of handsome volumes makes you want to pick up a glass of brandy and brandish a cue, and the dining room is the sort of place where you want to congregate with your friends over a weekend dinner – couscous salad with local seafood; roast monkfish with vegetables; barbary duck with a peanut stuffing – transforming the time and place into a country house weekend.

● **OPEN:**
Mar 1-end Oct
(house parties accepted off season)
● **ROOMS:**
Five rooms. All en-suite
● **AVERAGE PRICE:**
B&B £30 per person sharing
£10 single supplement

● **NOTES:**
Dinner 8pm, £15-£18 separate tables
No Wheelchair Access
Children – welcome, high chairs, cots, babysitting.
Enclosed car parking
● From Waterford, take road to Tramore, past golf club on coast road to Dungarvan. Annestown is 51/2 miles west of Tramore.

BUGGY'S GLENCAIRN INN
Ken & Cathleen Buggy
Glencairn, Co Waterford
Tel: (058) 56232

There are certain people in Ireland whose style is so distinctive that it defines everything about their work. Not only is it intensely personal, but it is so organic and natural that it is impossible for others to imitate it. A man no-one could imitate is Ken Buggy.

His style is utterly unmistakable, both in his manner and in how he shapes and decorates a space. He loves irony and contrast, loves salvage and counterpoint, he loves – in short – being different, and no one could complement his style more than Cathleen Buggy with her patient, quiet nature. Their combined style has made Buggy's Glencairn Inn unique.

It is a lovely little house, dating back to 1720, but it wears its years lightly. There is a little bar downstairs, quite unlike any other bar in Ireland. There is a small dining room, and three bedrooms upstairs.

The rooms are idiosyncratic, pell-mell and pristine, a kaleidoscope of Ken Buggy's work as artist and collector. Their assemblage of artefact and comfort is unlike any other house, and the second you set eyes on these big, beautiful beds in their cosy, low-ceilinged rooms, you want to swaddle in their capacious linens, sleep the good sleep.

● **OPEN:**
All year
No dinner Tue, Nov-Feb, but good local facilities
● **ROOMS:**
Three rooms, all en-suite
● **AVERAGE PRICE:**
B&B £28-£30 per person sharing
£8 single supplement

● **NOTES:**
Dinner from 6.30pm, £16-£20, booking advisable
Off street car parking
No Wheelchair Access
Children – welcome but no facilities
● In Lismore turn right at monument, drive to
Horneybrooks garage where you will see sign for
Glencairn, turn right, 3 miles.

①

ADELE'S
SCHULL, CO CORK

②

ARDNAMONA
LOUGH ESKE, CO DONEGAL

③

BERRYHILL
INISTIOGE, CO KILKENNY

④

ECHO LODGE
BALLINGARRY, CO LIMERICK

⑤

ISKEROON
CAHERDANIEL, CO KERRY

⑥

LISS ARD LAKE LODGE
SKIBBEREEN, CO CORK

⑦

THE MORGAN
DUBLIN, CO DUBLIN

⑧

SALVILLE HOUSE
ENNISCORTHY, CO WEXFORD

⑨

SCILLY HOUSE INN
KINSALE, CO CORK

⑩

SHELBURNE LODGE
KENMARE, CO KERRY

HANORA'S COTTAGE
Seamus & Mary Wall
Nire Valley, Clonmel, Co Waterford
Tel: (052) 36134
Fax: 36540

In Hanora's Cottage, every member of the Wall family plays their part in creating what is one of the best escapes in the country.

Let's take breakfast, for example. Arrayed on a table will be bowls of poached nectarines, bowls of apricots, bowls of prunes, special porridge and there will be a phalanx of other cereals as well, three varieties of Dick and Anne Keating's smashing Baylough cheese, ripe melons, good apples, nutty brown bread, squidgy scones, juicy plums, white batch loaf, smoked salmon, fresh juices, rich, thick cream.

And, then, Mrs Wall will walk in, and ask you what you would like for breakfast! Don't miss the good scrambled eggs, and the sweet bacon. Some good coffee, and you are off to the best start to the day ever.

It is evening. You have pounded those hills and valleys. And now young Eoin Wall takes over, and produces a great dinner: some chicken and bacon sausage with a red onion marmalade; poached fillet of salmon with a herb butter, and a good gratin of courgettes and tomatoes to set beside the floury spuds. Then a good fruit pudding, and a fine bottle of wine. Bed beckons, sweetly, blissfully. Bliss.

● **OPEN:**
All year, except Christmas
● **ROOMS:**
Six rooms
Four with jacuzzi bath,
2 with bathrooms
● **AVERAGE PRICE:**
B&B £35-£40 per person sharing
£10 single supplement

● **NOTES:**
Dinner 6.30pm–9pm, £20
No Wheelchair Access
No children
Off street car parking
● From Clonmel or Dungarvan, follow signs to
Ballymaclery village, the House is signposted from there.

RICHMOND HOUSE
Paul & Claire Deevy
Cappoquin
Co Waterford
Tel: (058) 54278
Fax: 54988
website: http://www.amireland.com/richmond

There are many nice things one can say to explain just how nice a place Richmond House is.

Nice food, cooked with care and panache by Paul Deevy. Nice service in the restaurant, by local ladies and by Paul's wife, Claire. Nice public rooms, for having a drink before dinner, or lounging with a cup of coffee in front of the fire. Nice bedrooms, simple, a little old-fashioned. The house is nicely situated, close to Cappoquin, and a good base for exploring this terrific, rather neglected part of Waterford county. It's a handsome house, 300 years old, but spick and span and dapper inside as the Deevy family, who have been here for 30 years, steadily put their plans into operation each year.

And then it strikes you that what is nice about Richmond House is, well... its niceness. It's an unselfconscious niceness. A generous niceness. A comfy niceness. A personable niceness. It's not a twee niceness, or a sham niceness. Instead it's real, true, genuine. It's a very Irish niceness. This is what we do, it says. This is how the family run the house and the restaurant. We hope you like it. And you will, that's for sure.

● **OPEN:**
Feb–Xmas
● **ROOMS:**
Nine rooms, all en-suite
● **AVERAGE PRICE:**
B&B £35–£50 per person sharing
£10 single supplement

● **NOTES:**
Dinner 7pm-9pm, £27
Wheelchair Access
Children – welcome, high chairs and cots
Enclosed car parking
● From Waterford take the N25 to Dungarvan, then from Cappoquin the House is signposted on the left hand side of the road.

CROOKEDWOOD HOUSE

Noel & Julie Kenny
Crookedwood, Mullingar
Co Westmeath
Tel: (044) 72165 Fax: 72166
cwoodhse@iol.ie

They are an impressive pair, Noel and Julie Kenny. Neither of them hail from the county – Mr Kenny is a Sligo man, his wife comes from just up the road in Longford – but it was discovering this lovely old parish rectory in Westmeath which brought them here, to Crookedwood, close to the magical waters of Lough Derravaragh, a potent stretch of water which is the setting for the story of Leda and the swans, and which can be seen from some of the bedrooms.

Over the years they have toiled away, bringing themselves to the position of pre-eminent restaurateurs in the county, and indeed elevating Mr Kenny to the position of one of the best known skillet-handlers in the country. He also effectively runs the kitchen by himself, whilst Mrs Kenny takes care of the front of house with authoritative calm. There are 8 well appointed rooms to the rear of the 18th century house, and they are a perfect base for exploring this neglected area, with all its overlooked attractions: the occluded light that dresses down the bogs, the early-morning mists which drape the fields like a spectral mantilla, the torrential rush of water which announces the power of the Shannon.

● **OPEN:**
All year, except Xmas
● **ROOMS:**
Eight rooms, all en-suite
● **AVERAGE PRICE:**
B&B £40-£50 per person sharing
£5 single supplement

● **NOTES:**
Dinner 7pm-10pm, £23, separate tables
No Wheelchair Access
Children – high chair, cot, babysitter
● Take 3rd exit off Mullingar by-pass, signed Castlepollard. Drive to Crookedwood village. Turn right at Wood pub, then 1.5 miles further along you will see the house.

TEMPLE

Declan & Bernadette Fagan
Horseleap, Moate, Co Westmeath
Tel: (0506) 35118
Fax: 35118
e-mail: temple@iol.ie

Temple is a monument dedicated to the God-who-gets-away-from-it-all. It is only half a mile from the main Dublin-Galway road, yet it feels like it is a million miles from anywhere. Few other houses in Ireland can maintain the conspiracy of perfect peace and relaxation you find here. You walk through the door, and you walk into another world. Immaculate housekeeping, spontaneous friendliness, and splendiferous cooking. Here is a house in which to have the time of your life.

But if Temple feels removed, its character nevertheless feels unassailably rooted in County Westmeath, and nothing creates this feeling more than Mrs Fagan's cooking.

"We wanted to continue the tradition of fine farm foods we were reared on", says Declan Fagan, and Bernadette's cooking is a triumph of regional creativity: local meats of superlative flavour from Tormey's of Mullingar, local dairy products and local fruits and vegetables are harnessed by Mrs Fagan's dedication to flavour. And boy!, does she make bumper puddings.

They have created a new Temple Spa in the courtyard, with a sauna, steamroom, hydrotherapy bath and massage and beauty rooms, and five new ensuite bedrooms upstairs, another dynamic and progressive step for one of the mot loveable, special houses in the country.

● **OPEN:**
Mar-Nov
● **ROOMS:**
Four rooms, all en-suite
● **AVERAGE PRICE:**
B&B £30 per person sharing
£10 single supplement

● **NOTES:**
Dinner 8pm, £10, communal table
No Wheelchair Access
Children – welcome, high chair, cot
● Half mile off the N6, clearly signposted,
1 mile west of Horseleap/4 miles east of Moate.

DUNBRODY COUNTRY HOUSE HOTEL

Kevin & Catherine Dundon
Arthurstown, New Ross, Co Wexford
Tel: (051) 389600
Fax: 389601
e-mail: dunbrody@indigo.ie

They do not want for confidence, Kevin and Catherine Dundon, who currently and actively restoring Dunbrody House to its former splendour.

They run the house in tandem with a fine, large restaurant, and if at present it feels like a work-in-progress, no one should doubt that they will succeed in their considerable challenge. Steadily and surely all the details will be put right – paintings by local artists instead of prints; finishing details in bathrooms; the abolition of part-baked bread (their own is so much better that they don't need that stuff).

Indeed, part of the fun of Dunbrody is seeing the relish they have for the challenge, the way in which they are learning the skills of housekeepers to place alongside those of the high-powered chef.

Already the grounds are being cleared to make space for herb and vegetable gardens, and a state of self-sufficiency will make Kevin Dundon's powerful and impressive cooking even better. Its location two hours from Dublin should attract a lot of weekenders to Dunbrody in the future, and they are planning various classes and courses as extra attractions. As a base for exploring this glorious part of the sunny south east, it couldn't be better.

● **OPEN:**
All year
● **ROOMS:**
Ten rooms, all en-suite. Two suites
● **AVERAGE PRICE:**
B&B from £45 per person sharing
£10 single supplement

● **NOTES:**
Dinner 8pm, from £20
Full Wheelchair Access
Children – welcome, high chair, cot
● From Wexford, you pass the house on the left hand side, going down the hill into Arthurstown.

FURZIESTOWN HOUSE
Yvonne Pim
Tacumshane, Co Wexford
Tel: (053) 31376

Furziestown is a cutely nice farmhouse, set way, way down there in the heel of the country that is south Wexford, the sunny south-east, and it is the right house in the right place: comfortable, friendly, understated, hard to leave.

The intuitive thoughtfulness which Yvonne Pim brings to everything about the house, and Mrs Pim's care and concern for her guests, makes the house someplace special. Someplace special be damned! This is one of the most highly regarded places to stay in the country. Without even trying, you will find that you love it.

And you will love the breakfasts, which reflect not just an environmentally sensitive cook, but a cook whose feel for flavour is unwaveringly exact. Mrs Pim's fruit compotes are special, her granola is special, her eggs – collected from hens who wander around the yard outside in communion with lots of other happy, healthy farmyard animals, including an amorous turkey – are spankingly fresh, and there are thoughtful variations for vegetarians.

Many travellers who stay their first night with Mrs Pim find that they must spend their last night at Furziestown also. Mrs Pim's house allows us a microcosm of all that is good about Irish hospitality.

● **OPEN:**
May-Nov
● **ROOMS:**
Two rooms
Both en-suite
● **AVERAGE PRICE:**
B&B from £18 per person

● **NOTES:**
No Dinner
No Wheelchair Access
Children – welcome, high chair, cot, baby listening
From Wexford take N25 heading for Rosslare.
At Killinick turn right and right again in front of the Merry Elf pub. Follow road approx 2 miles to T junction. Turn left following sign for Tacumshane. Continue until you see sign for house.

KELLY'S RESORT HOTEL ✪
Bill Kelly
Rosslare
Co Wexford
Tel: (053) 32114
Fax: 32222
e-mail: kellyhot@iol.ie
website: http://www.kellys.ie

Kelly's Resort Hotel is a place where everything – the works of art, the service, the style, the concern, the affability, the cooking – works to lift your spirits.

The hotel puts you on your best behaviour, not through any strictures, but simply by example. I'm worth this, you reckon to yourself, and it is a classic example of virtue breeding virtue, a moral method of making the perfect guests in the perfect hotel.

The Kelly family have had more than a century to practice their craft, but Bill Kelly and his team have a spring in their step which shows how much they love their work. Nothing is a cliché, from a correctly served breakfast through to the mid-morning cup of tea, then a buffet lunch and, after a swim and a stroll to try to keep in shape, a delicious dinner in the grand dining room before you sleep the good sleep.

The addition of La Marine Bistro, where Eugene Callaghan cooks, gives another essential distraction, but it is possible to come to Kelly's for a week and never set foot outside this republic of pleasure. It is an inspiring place, an Irish classic, and quite unique and memorable.

● **OPEN:**
late Feb-early Dec
● **ROOMS:**
Ninety nine rooms, all en-suite
● **AVERAGE PRICE:**
B&B £40-£65+10% per person sharing
£3 single supplement

● **NOTES:**
Dinner 7.30pm-9pm, £22 +10%
Full Wheelchair Access
Children – welcome, high chair, cot
● Take the N25 from Dublin to Rosslare. Hotel situated in Rosslare Strand.

McMENAMIN'S TOWNHOUSE
Seamus & Kay McMenamin
3 Auburn Terrace, Redmond Road, Wexford,
Co Wexford
Tel: (053) 46442

If there is one single element which remains with you after a stay at Seamus and Kay McMenamins' friendly and efficacious house, it is the generosity which underpins everything they do.

Ask a question about this delightful town or the delightful county, and you will be told all you need to know, and likely a bit more besides.

State an affection for some particular breakfast dish – some fish, maybe, or a necklace of rum to ring around your porridge, or a particular type of bread – and it will be brought to life next morning, all the better to delight you. Indeed, the staggering choice of foods available at breakfast is almost overwhelming in its largesse: a bumper of breads, fruits, juices, eggs, steaming coffee and wake-up tea are arrayed before you, a breakfast perfectly described by visitors from Down Under as "phenomenal".

The collection of beds which grace the various rooms, some of them of very great value, add an extra sheen to the house, which works brilliantly as a base for first night-last night stays, thanks to its proximity to Rosslare, but is also perfect for the Opera Festival, and for enjoyably aimless meandering through the Sunny South-East.

● **OPEN:**
All year, except Xmas
● **ROOMS:**
Six rooms,
all en-suite
● **AVERAGE PRICE:**
B&B £22.50 per person
£27 single occupancy

● **NOTES:**
No Dinner
No Wheelchair Access
Locked parking
Children – welcome, high chair, cot, babysitting
● Near the bus & rail stations.

SALVILLE HOUSE →
Jane & Gordon Parker
Enniscorthy, Co Wexford
Tel: (054) 35252 Fax: 35252

If someone suggested to you that the following was an evening menu at Alice Waters' celebrated San Francisco restaurant, Chez Panisse, you might say: "Of course. Such simplicity. And the green salad with the tarragon chicken, a typical touch", and you might hope to some day be able to eat something so profound.

Croghan goat's cheese and sun-dried tomato toasts; Yellow pepper soup; Tarragon chicken, straw potatoes, green salad; Plum and apple crumble; Coffee or tea.

It's not Chez Panisse, but Salville House, and the kind of dinner which Jane and Gordon Parker prepare in their utterly lovely home, just south of Enniscorthy.

Such a clever, composed menu is typical of the choices the Parkers make, typical of their good judgement, and typical also of their understated style. No flowery, unnecessary language, no archness, no conceit. Just the kind of noble cooking you dream of coming across in a beautiful house like Salville.

Like the cooking, the beauty here consists of placing the right thing in the right context. It is a simple house, elegant, very personal, original, quiet, but its position, high on a hill overlooking the Slaney River, is perfect, almost as if it belongs in a painting. Delightful.

● **OPEN:**
All year
● **ROOMS:**
Three rooms. two en suite, one with private
one private apartment
● **AVERAGE PRICE:**
B&B £22.50 per person sharing
£5 single supplement
private apartment priced seasonally

● **NOTES:**
Dinner, £18, communal table
Wheelchair Access to private apartment only
Children – welcome, high chair, cot
● Just off the N11 to Wexford — take the first left
after the hospital, go up the hill to a T-junction then turn
left and proceed for one third of a mile.

THE OLD RECTORY
Paul and Linda Saunders
Wicklow, Co Wicklow
Tel: (0404) 67048 Fax: 69181
mail@oldrectory.ie

It is painted pink outside and, with the exception of the dining and drawing rooms, The Old Rectory is an otherwise distinctly feminine house. Whilst Paul Saunders is, obviously, one of the twin pillars of the house, it is Linda Saunders who supplies the mettle of the Rectory.

She does this not just by her quiet thoroughness, though the attention to every detail in The Old Rectory is dauntless, but principally through her wonderful cooking. Using organic ingredients and bringing to them a skillfulness which can offer balance and expressiveness in a meal, Mrs Saunders is one of the best country house cooks.

And her food steers well clear of the animal-fat and carbohydrate syndrome so beloved of these big old piles. The vegetarian dinners Linda prepares, in particular, are artful, ingenious, painstaking. Quaff some of the unexpected varietals of Spanish wine which Paul Saunders has to hand and you have an evening to remember.

The house is colourfully furnished, with warm pastels and comforting paintings, the bedrooms opting for soft light and colours whilst the sitting-room and dining room tend to greater formality. The addition of new rooms and a gym for sporty types rounds out a complete little place.

● **OPEN:**
Mar-Dec
● **ROOMS:**
Seven rooms
All en-suite
● **AVERAGE PRICE:**
B&B £50 per person sharing
£25 single supplement

● **NOTES:**
Dinner 8pm, £29.50
Enclosed car parking
No Wheelchair Access
Children – welcome, high chair, cot, baby listening
● From Dublin take N211 to Rathnew, then R750 to Wicklow Town. Entrance on left, marked by stone walls, 100 yds after Jet Garage. 5 miles from railway station.

RATHSALLAGH HOUSE
Joe and Kay O'Flynn
Dunlavin
Co Wicklow
Tel: (045) 53112
Fax: 53343

People enjoy themselves in Rathsallagh. Indeed, one of the accidental pleasures of the house is to observe just how its guests appreciate and exploit the luxuries which Rathsallagh offers.

Seeing the busy behaviour of the guests at breakfast, milling around the dishes on the sideboard, agonising over what gargantuan helpings of the various options they should help themselves to, you would imagine everyone was getting everything free, such is their air of unconcerned joyousness. Seeing them stroll around the grand grounds, as early morning mists lift and reveal the splendours of the gardens, they are people at peace.

But then it is probably the skillfulness of Joe and Kay O'Flynn in setting a mood of unconcerned relaxation which helps people to forget the price of everything and concentrate instead on the value of having a fine time. The house itself is an abiding collection of converted stables set in massive and distinctively mature grounds, and everything conspires to set the agenda for away-from-it-all fun, a vivacious and vicious sense of spoil-yourself-you-deserve-it luxury. It is terribly easy to like Rathsallagh, and easy to feel that you need to scoot out of Dublin right now and wind up here to wind down.

● **OPEN:**
All year, except Xmas
● **ROOMS:**
Seventeen rooms, all en-suite
● **AVERAGE PRICE:**
B&B £55-£95 per person sharing
£30-£50 single supplement

● **NOTES:**
Dinner £30-£35, separate tables
Enclosed car park
No Wheelchair Access
Children – over 12yrs welcome
● Signposted in Dunlavin village, 1 hour from Dublin

TINAKILLY HOUSE HOTEL
William & Bee Power
Rathnew, Co Wicklow
Tel: (0404) 69274 Fax: 67806
e-mail: wpower@tinakilly.ie
website: http://www.tinakilly.ie

Bill Power is the man responsible for Tinakilly. He is a fabulous hotel keeper, a man who can inspire his staff with the merest urging, someone whose decorum might almost belong to a bygone age. Except his reserve, and his correctness, is bright and busy and functioning in Tinakilly day after day, cracking this big old pile of a place along with the hum of a Bugatti, seeing everything is right.

His lieutenants in the business of running a superlative hotel are his wife, Bee, and his staff, who fuse efficiency with charm as if they had taken it in with mother's milk.

The key players in recent years in Tinakilly have been John Moloney's team in the kitchen, and together they have almost revitalised the concept of hotel food.

There is both grace and inventiveness in the cooking: warm salad of duck with aubergine relish and blueberries; escalopes of salmon with a feuillete of winter vegetables; loin of lamb with a potato and leek galette; pheasant with celeriac mash. Good food, assuredly delivered.

Christmas at Tinakilly, by the way, is splendid, and breakfast in bed on Sunday morning is one of the great treats to be enjoyed in Ireland.

● **OPEN:**
All year
● **ROOMS:**
Forty one rooms. All en-suite
● **AVERAGE PRICE:**
B&B £60-£85 per person sharing
£40 single supplement

● **NOTES:**
Dinner 7.30pm-9pm, £30
Private car parking
Full Wheelchair Access
Children – welcome, high chair, cot
● Take N11 south from Dublin. Bear left in Rathnew village. The house is 500 yds on left as you drive towards Wicklow town.

NORTHERN IRELAND

ASH ROWAN
Evelyn & Sam Hazlett
12 Windsor Avenue, Belfast, BT9 6EE, Northern Ireland
Tel: (01232) 661985 Fax: 663227

Sam and Evelyn. This is what the Ash Rowan is all about, and discovering this is something you discover the second you walk through the door.

Sam and Evelyn greet and meet, advise and cook, chat and speculate, gossip and inform. After about 90 seconds you reckon you have known them for half your life

It's no surprise, then, that the road-weary crew who are the classical musicians of the world, and other performers, should so assiduously colonise the Ash Rowan when they are here for the Belfast festival.

So, the Ash Rowan, with its politely understated decor, its slightly distressed grouting which is just like home, its element of mix-match and steady accumulation, its collation of private memorabilia arranged here and there, is a house where it is easy to lay your head.

Evelyn is a good cook, and a woman with a very true appreciation of good food. Breads, coffee and - above all - her scrambled eggs, enjoy the sure touch of someone who loves food and can't tolerate doing something by rote. It is the final element in a house which has the sort of relaxed character that makes you want to linger for a few days, thanks to Sam and Evelyn.

● **OPEN:**
all year, except Xmas
● **ROOMS:**
Five rooms, all en-suite
● **AVERAGE PRICE:**
B&B £33-£36 per person sharing
£10 single supplement

● **NOTES:**
Dinner 7pm, £25, separate tables
Locked car parking
No Wheelchair Access
Children – over 12 yrs welcome
● From city centre take Dublin road to Shaftesbury Square, then through Bradbury Place on to University road. Windsor Ave is the 3rd Ave on right past the Botanic Inn.

HALCYON HOUSE

Mary & John Potter
68 Wellington Park, Malone Road
Belfast BT9 6DP
Tel: (01232) 681648 Fax: 681648
mary@halcyon-house.demon.co.uk

Wellington Park was the road where Mary and John Potter always wanted to live – the couple met in a restaurant just around the corner – and even though both hail from County Fermanagh, they seem rooted in this nice, buzzy bourgeois part of Belfast. "We always felt connected to Wellington Park", says Mary. "We always liked the mix of architectural styles amongst the houses on the road".

Mary had always wanted to work at home, and offering rooms for B&B means that "I can be here, and do everything for the guests"

Word spreads quickly when you are good at your job, and Mrs Potter is rather good. She is loquacious, instantly friendly, welcoming. The troupe from The Irish Times were amongst the first to arrive, reporters up from Dublin covering the various non-events of Northern Irish politics, folk doubtless glad of a cosy sitting room to return to, and a good breakfast to set them up in the morning before they headed off for a day of soundbites.

And others have followed, keen to cultivate their space in this friendly house, so that most business in Halcyon is return business, the best guarantee you can get that someone is doing something right.

Halcyon's location is, of course, superb, with the centre of Belfast no more than a few minute's walk away.

● **OPEN:**
All year, except Xmas
● **ROOMS:**
Two rooms, share one bathroom & two toilets
● **AVERAGE PRICE:**
B&B £20 per person sharing
£23-£25 single

● **NOTES:**
No Dinner
No private car park. No Wheelchair Access
Children – welcome, high chair, cot
● Between the Lisburn and Malone road.

MADDYBENNY FARM HOUSE
Rosemary White
18 Maddybenny Park, Portrush
Co Antrim
Tel: (01265) 823394
Fax: 823394

It is a mark of just how famous and respected Rosemary White's cooking is that a great baker and writer such as Linda Collister should choose Mrs White's recipe for fadge – local potato bread – to include in her great work, "The Bread Book". Ms Collister quotes an adjudicator in the Great Irish Breakfast Awards as saying, "her breakfast was magnificent, and the presentation faultless".

And indeed it is. Breakfast in the cosy, comfy Maddybenny Farmhouse is an epic adventure, an inventory of all the foods that can be enjoyed first thing in the morning: porridge with Drambuie; a big fry-up with that famous fadge and soda bread; kipper fillets with dill; lamb's kidneys; scrambled eggs, you name it. Nothing is left out, everything is possible.

And Mrs White's secret is simple: "I never start to cook for my guests in the morning till I see the whites of their eyes", she says, and she works hard to keep Maddybenny in tip-top shape, recently adding self-catering cottages, and running a riding centre from the farm. It all adds up to a great base from which to explore this magnificent coastline, and there are fine local restaurants. But don't miss the fadge.

● **OPEN:**
All year, except Xmas
● **ROOMS:**
Three rooms, all en-suite
Six self catering cottages also available
● **AVERAGE PRICE:**
B&B £25 per person sharing

● **NOTES:**
No Dinner
Enclosed parking
No Wheelchair Access
Children – welcome, high chair, cot
● At the A29 Coleraine/Portrush road you will see a sign for Maddybenny Riding Centre, B&B and Holiday Cottages

THE NARROWS

Will & James Brown
8 Shore Road, Portaferry
Co Down BT22 1JY
Tel: (012477) 28148 Fax: 28105
e-mail: the.narrows@dial.pipex.com
website: http://www.nova.co.uk./nova/strngfrd/
narrow1.htm

There is something splendidly refreshing and enlivening when you first encounter a house which has forged and furnished its own solutions to its own design problems. The Narrows is just such a house.

Time and again, in rooms of differing sizes and shapes, there are clever touches which solve the difficulties of agonies such as the shower room in the corner or the low ceiling, smart ideas which allow for panoramic perspectives from dormer windows, which exploit light sources to give contrast to rooms, which allow the buildings to switch from private to public without any tension, and which at the same time never neglects to exploit one of the glories of the location – the glinting slip of water which wraps around Portaferry and Strangford and which is only metres away from the front of the house.

In designation, the Narrows falls between several stools, being neither guest house, hotel, nor hostel. Its originality is the real pleasure of the place, that and the fact that the brothers Brown work so hard, with their most recent move being to purloin a pair of chefs who worked with Robbie Millar, in Shanks, all the better to upgrade the food they can offer in The Narrows. This is a significant step, and a vital pointer to the ambition of The Narrows.

● **OPEN:**
All year
● **ROOMS:**
Thirteen rooms, all en-suite
● **AVERAGE PRICE:**
B&B £33 per person sharing
£5 single supplement

● **NOTES:**
Lunch (£10) and Dinner (£17) Mon-Sun
Full Wheelchair Access
Children – welcome, high chair, cot
● On the seafront at Portaferry

STREEVE HILL
Peter & June Welch
Limavady, Co Londonderry, BT49 OHP
Tel: (015047) 66563
Fax: 68285

"As the tyres of your car sink into the deep gravel forecourt of this deceptively large Palladian dower house, it is abundantly clear that, for this moment in time at least, this is where you belong".

This is how a friend described arriving at Streeve. He wasn't even in the door of June and Peter Welch's house and he felt he belonged!

They are experts at the game of hospitality, with their care centred firmly on meticulous attention to detail: a judicious assembly of antique furniture, a generous hand with the pre-dinner drinks, fresh flowers, crisp linen, and their style is adroitly helpful, never intrusive, well judged, and thus enjoyably relaxing.

Mrs Welch is an expert in the kitchen, confident with her ingredients, her food full of graceful notes and gestures. But then the cooking is just another element of the search for perfection that animates Streeve. Homemade croissants for breakfast, with an array of compotes and confitures, pinhead oatmeal porridge on the hot plate, kidneys and rashers, copious coffee.

"There is no sense of being hurried", said our friend. "I had the impression that we could have lingered as long as we wanted". This is the spell the Welchs weave.

● **OPEN:**
All year, except Xmas and New Year
● **ROOMS:**
Two double bedrooms, one twin room, all with private bathrooms
● **AVERAGE PRICE:**
B&B £35-£45 per person sharing
£5 single supplement

● **NOTES:**
Dinner 8pm, £25, separate tables
No Wheelchair Access
Children – welcome, high chair, cot
● From Limavady take the A2 to Castlerock. On leaving the town the Estate wall is on the right, 200 yds past the Gate Lodge turn right up the lane

GRANGE LODGE
Norah Brown
Grange Rd
Dungannon
Co Tyrone
Tel: (018687) 84212
Fax: 723891

What is most especially enjoyable about Norah Brown's cooking in Grange Lodge Country House, a fine Georgian house just a stone's throw from the M1 motorway, is the fact that it represents the perfection of domestic cookery. The food is simple, direct, delicious, and in this cosy big house it suits your moods and needs just perfectly.

The pleasure of sitting down in the small dining room in Grange and eating dinner gives joy to both body and soul. And what, then, do your thoughts turn to the instant dinner is over? To breakfast, no less, and a bowl of porridge that may have already begun its long overnight simmer in the oven.

In the morning, it will receive the expert ministrations of Ralph Brown as he first scatters crystals of brown sugar on top, then annotates the soft grains with a generous splash of Bushmills whiskey before a cloak of rich cream melds with the sugar and the hooch. From first mouthful, you are in culinary heaven, the pleasure points in your body reaching some sort of frothy ferment, a ferment maintained by a generous and expert Ulster Fried breakfast. Grange is a mavellous base for exploring, and for returning.

● **OPEN:**
Feb-20 Dec
● **ROOMS:**
Five rooms, all en-suite
● **AVERAGE PRICE:**
B&B £34.50 per person sharing
£49 single occupancy

● **NOTES:**
Dinner 7.30pm-9pm, £22
No Wheelchair Access
Children – over 10 yrs welcome
● From M1 junction 15 take the A29 to Armagh. After 1 mile turn left at sign, Grange, after 200 metres fork right and the house is first set of white pillars on right

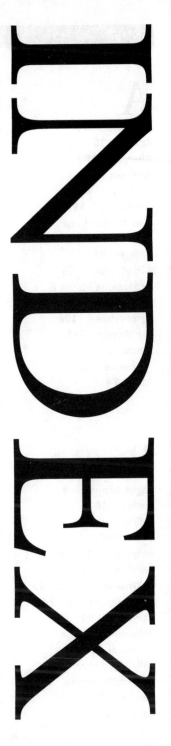